BETTER LEFT
AS
MEMORIES

Sequel to Between the Highway and the Fence Post

E.C. HERBERT

For information contact: info@outlawspublishing.com
Cover Design by Outlaws Publishing LLC
Edited by Ann Mealler Grigsby
Published by Outlaws Publishing LLC
July 202410 9 8 7 6 5 4 3 2 1

PROLOGUE

Fifty years! That's half-a-century, two-hundred seasons, that's how long it had been since I graduated from high school back in 1968, and along with a fellow hippie sat out across the country bound for California's Haight Ashbury, and Golden Gate Park, and to visit with my brother by way of the famous Route 66, the *Mother Road*, as it had come to be known.

We hitched it in its entirety. To this day I haven't met another person who had done that.

I met those who hitched to California, but not the entire Route 66.

Route 66, a route that I'd washed windows and pumped gas in probably every gas station located on it to get enough money for some needed food, and maybe a joint or two.

Two McDonald's cheeseburgers, fries, and a coke, then thumbs out to continue our pilgrimage across the country.

Remembered days filled with sunshine, and good times.

This trek of 1968 I have given snap-shots to in the novel, Between the White Line and the Fence Post, a journey where my mind was often clouded over by the drugs of the day or alcohol, so you can see my excitement when I learned that two high school brothers were planning a trip to California following Route 66, and visiting all the sights that were left to visit for a chance to hopefully step- back-in-time, and experience a simpler way of life if only for a few days, but no drugs or booze would cloud over my mind on this trip, and I was excited to experience my own fifty year flash-back-in-time.

One phone call to my high school buddies, and I had weaseled my way onto the back seat of their vehicle, and into an adventure both exciting, happy, and at times bittersweet with my face pressed up to the window gazing out onto a land I once hiked in, and silent tears would roll down my cheek, neck, and soak the front of my tee shirt at times.

At these times I wondered what my friends up front were thinking as they looked out over what was once many flourishing businesses of the sixties, now all dead shells of twenty-eighteen, and I got to thinking how much this related to our own mortality.

When asked if I planned on writing a book documenting this trip, I knew that I wanted to, I just didn't know which way I would write it.

At first it was going to be a book of reliving old memories, revisiting old sights, and places I could remember.

Places I had walked over. Places I had pumped gas in, washed windows in, swept out floors in, and re-calling the stories I would tell them of our journey, and watch the expressions on their faces as I would re-tell the time I had spent with the little flower girl, under an overpass during a pounding rain storm, that I'd met someplace along the way.

But these days were different.

Gone was the need to pump gas or wash windows to earn a few dollars to buy burgers and fries, and to advance our trip.

Gone also was the desire for that little flower girl.

Who knows? She was probably the middle aged women taking my money for the bag a goodies I had just purchased at the gas/convenient store, something that the trip of 1968 didn't have.

For a passing moment though, I smiled to myself wondering if she could have been. Shaking off the thought, I took my change and thanked her, as much for the goodies, as well as for a 50 year old memory.

Gone was the want for drugs, and alcohol to cloud over my mind, replaced instead with the desire to remember as much as I could of those pasted years, and to be able to relate them to the present.

Some of those gas stations and businesses had been re-furbished to their glory days and I wondered now if they were ones I had pumped gas in or washed windows in. This lack of memory would set my thoughts in a different direction.

In mentioning my dilemma to my daughter-in-law Kari, she reminded me of something I had told her before she became my daughter-in-law.

Old boyfriends are old boyfriends for a reason, I had told her when talking about an old boyfriend coming back into her life. Kari also had just met our son Kevin who she wanted to get to know, now these words of advice rang out in my memory as plain as I remembered the very day I had said them.

Old clouded over memories are old clouded over memories for a reason.

This brought a smile to my face as I looked upon her figure standing there, and now the gas station, and knew exactly how I would write this book if memories came back to me, or at the time thought I would.

Nothing could prepare me for the dark memoires that would surface.

Back to that day, Kari made the decision to leave an old boyfriend, and memories of old days for new memories to be had, with a new boyfriend and future husband, my son.

Over the years, and three children later, I know Kari has never once regretted her decision.

So, how to relate.

Instead of trying to remember the past, which one cannot change, I would look for new things and experiences to store and recall in a new book to be hopefully enjoyed by all you readers, but the past would come alive!

At times, old memories would pop-up, but I would put them away and turn them around into new ones connecting the two, especially if it turned out to be a refurbished business who had fought to survive the years, and now stood, still alive.

Old memories wouldn't be put away or turned around!

New products adorned their shelves, and the faces were much younger than the fifty or so years it had lived, but it had survived the years.

Just like we do. We marry and have kids, not so much to grow up and be like us, but to forge their own roads in life, and if by chance they choose to follow in our footsteps they will still evolve into their individual selves, with their children carrying on after them.

So, here is a new refurbished gas station. We as parents are gone and replaced by our children, the new station. The old shell having been given a face lift, and their children, relating to the new products on the shelves, continuing on, leaving the old behind and making a new, built up from the same shell, and hopefully those new products on the shelves would someday be replaced by new one also, as another line grows up.

Old clouded over memories would now be just that….Old clouded over memories.

A new refurbished mind would take in all the new sights. A mind which might still remember the past, just as our memories recall our parents, but now with a mind living in the today, taking in all of the today sights.

From Presidents Lincoln Tomb to the Santa Monica Pier we drove Route 66 as much as we could.

Many business were gone just like our lives do. We come to the end then we are gone from sight. Many businesses stood as empty, broken down shells, a remembrance to our present life. Our aged bodies just like the gas station broken down but still adorning a space on this earth refusing to die and leave it.

Then the new one. This a living sign contesting to our heritage. Now all grown up and making its own way in the world, just like our children, and grandchildren do sometime follow in out footsteps, or stepping onto their own path and leaving their own footsteps.

This story will have many strange, and at times dark twist, I hope you all enjoy.

CHAPTER 1

The email from an old friend caught my attention. It was from my old time friend and fellow class mate from the Laconia High School who I will call Ern. Ern and I had been best friend for as long as I can remember, and when we got our driver license the need for speed, and fast cars, was born.

Neither Ern nor I were avid readers, but the JC Whitney automotive parts catalog occupied our back seat.

Duel Thrush Mufflers made my car one of the loudest in the city and I never passed up the opportunity to clutch my car into neutral, *revvvvve* up the motor, and listen to the loud *dadadadadada* as those duel Thrush Mufflers sang their song reverberating through the church organ pipes I backed them up with, as I drifted by a cop car who had another car pulled over, and saw his look of despair in my rear view mirror as I passed, and would gave him a wave of the hand.

My actions of course held re-actions from the Laconia Police.

Ern's mom would get a kick out of listening to my stories, while his dad would simple lower his head, shake it back and forth, and walk away causing us all to hoot, and howl.

These were the good-ole-days as most of us over the hill folk refer to them, and a time in Ern's life now he was looking to re-capture with this trip.

It was a hot Wednesday morning May 30th when Ern pulled into my dirt drive to pick me up. I had been up for many hours anxiously waiting his arrival.

It was a hot morning, and seeing I had left New Hampshire in June of 1968, I would guess the temperature in Fort Wayne, IN this morning was similar to what it had been in New Hampshire that morning fifty years ago.

It was a happy time seeing Ern and Big Bird again. Hugs, and loud sounding pats on the back. It had been about eight years since I had last seen them. Travel for my job had put me close enough to their place so I was able to visit for a couple of hours.

Introducing them to my wife, then loading the vehicle with my stuff, a quick kiss good-bye to the wifey, and our journey back to a different era in time was started. This excitement stayed with us all the way to the Santa Monica Pier, and the end of Route 66.

Ern, armed with a Route 66 hand guide, and his ever present cell phone, gave driving directions to Big Bird who would be the 1st to drive. I longed to be able to drive, and I didn't realize how hard it would become not being able to.

Oh! Big Bird was armed with his Tom-Tom whose voice was the most aggravating one for an electronic device Ern, and I have ever heard, and she kept getting lost.

I could tell I was going to have a hard time not grabbing it from its holder sitting up there pretty on the dash, and throwing it out an open window.

Her most used phrase being; *when possible make a U-turn.*

But, thru the whole trip I refrained from doing so, but at times fingers would be jammed tightly into my ears, and I would find myself slowly counting backward down from one-hundred.

Small price to pay for a trip like this, I told my mind whenever these times occurred, which became less, and less until our return trip where I found myself arguing with miss know it all Tom-Tom, as we neared the Illinois and Indiana border. This a story I will get into later.

At the start of our trip the decision was made not to drive into Chicago where officially Route 66 begins, but to start it in the Oak Ridge Cemetery located in Springfield, IL.

The tomb of our Sixteenth President Abraham Lincoln, and his Monument is located there, and a must see if in Springfield, IL and one Ern wanted to visit. Lincoln's Tomb was also in Ern's guide. When we were done we could easily pick-up Route 66, and continue on with our journey.

In all my US travel I had never visited this site and was happy it had been part of this trip. I stood somewhat in awe looking upon this glowing, gray, structure as the sun was basking down upon it giving it, its awesome glow.

Ern had purchased some kind of government pass which got us into all federal sites, sometimes free, and sometimes at a very low cost. It covered everyone in his group. A handicap parking permit topped it off allowing us close parking to the sites.

I was seeing the Lincoln Monument for the first time as well as Ern, and Big Bird, and I wondered if they were feeling some of the feelings I was. A brand new picture was formed in my memory that day which I will give you a slight description of. For more information along with a slew of pictures, visit the many web sites on Abraham Lincoln, but here is my nut-shell description.

The Lincoln Memorial was started in 1869 being completed in 1874. It was designed by Larkin Goldsmith Mead. It is constructed of cement with the entire interior being marble which was harvested from several US states along with, Italy, Spain, France, and Belgium. The exterior along with the interior display many statues. The last restoration was completed between the years 1930-31. Very little has been done to the memorial since then.

Besides the body of Abe Lincoln, his wife Mary Todd Lincoln with three of their sons are also buried there. Them being, Edward, William, and Thomas. Robert Todd being the only son not buried there.

In the front of the monument is a sculptured bust of Lincoln by Gutzon Borguim. The bust has a silver nose, which too many is considered lucky if rubbed.

I stood and witnessed many doing this with smiles on their faces. No doubt these smiles were brought on with thoughts of riches coming their way, or getting whatever they had wished for.

As I gazed upon everyone rubbing Lincoln's nose, low and behold if I didn't first see Ern doing this while being photographed by his brother, then the two traded place, and it was Big Birds time to rub, and get lucky. At this time, being prompted by both of them, I joined in also.

Later at the first gas stop, Big Bird went in and purchased a $5.00 scratch and won $100.00 bucks. Go figure! Me? Zeeeeeelch. Big Bird would later lose it all plus in the Route 66 Casino.

Having toured the inside, I went out into the hot, sunny day. The Oak Ridge Cemetery sure was a beautiful cemetery. One of the things I have enjoyed in past travels was stopping and visiting newly up-kept cemeteries, and old ones. Their un-mowed grass growing up and obscuring from anyone's view, the grave marker of wood or cement. Long gone were the names carved into them, the years taking its toll.

As with the newly mowed grasses of a well-manicured cemetery might look, there is also a beauty in that old, un-kept one. Oak Ridge Cemetery being the cemetery housing the sixteenth President of the United States, had its lawns well-kept along with all the landscaping.

Sitting there in the silence between tours, I couldn't help but think back to that dreaded day in our history, and wonder what the thoughts were of those close to Abe Lincoln were as they stood around his bedside and looked down at his dying body, listening in silence, as he took the last breathes he would ever take in his lifetime.

What would have been their thoughts as he passed from this lifetime while looking ahead into the future, and to a war that was still being fought? *What would have been my thought upon hearing Lincoln take his last breathe*, I wondered. *And in the silence of the room hear the words of Lincoln's Secretary of war Edwin M Stanton whisper; "**Now he belongs to the ages**."*

As I sat there in the hotness of the day, blanketed over by the shade offered to me from a stately maple tree, I watched groups of the next generation of possible leaders get off buses. As they departed their bus, many seemed almost mesmerized and stood just staring at the gray, glowing, monument, just like I had done an hour before. They would soon join a tour, and would learn things about our sixteenth President that text books don't tell us anymore. They would hear and read the famous Gettysburg Address, and learn it was Abraham Lincoln who started the Republican Party.

"Why doesn't the world want its generations growing up with as much truth and knowledge as possible of the past I questioned?" Pondering my thoughts further I questioned more, *"Is the past here the same as I had told Kari? The past was the past for a reason?"*

This thought I put down in my pad as one to ask my two traveling friends.

With this question, I now wish I had followed one of the groups and listened to their comments, or even took a couple of them aside and asked the question. But I hadn't.

More buses arrived along with cars of families, and my thought returned to wondering what they would learn here today, and what impact it would have, if any, on their futures.

"Is there a future president on one of those buses? Or maybe that fourteen or so year old girl walking hand, and hand with her mom, and dad, would she be our first female president?" I questioned out loud asking the stately oak tree.

Abraham Lincoln believed in this great country, and knew that anything was possible to achieve if you were willing to work for, and earn it. He himself was a living, walking testimony to that truth. That has never changed. It's the same today, but you have to work for it.

Here my thoughts took a different turn just thinking of what our country looked like then compared to what it looks like today. *The laws of the land sure were different back then,* I told myself.

Looking up into the softly whispering leaves of the mighty oak tree I smiled to myself thinking it had to be just a small tree starting its life when construction began on Lincoln's resting place, or maybe it hadn't yet been born.

Either one, I thought, it didn't really matter much to an oak tree, but to a generation of peoples, well, that's a different story.

The biggest issue during Abe Lincoln's Presidency was slavery, and although it lead to the Civil War you didn't have so many other issues dividing the country, or if there were you didn't hear about them. Nope. I don't believe parents worried about their children getting shot down in the town's streets by a rival gang, or their child discussing wanting to be a girl, or a boy, or wanting to take one of their own sex into marriage. Sure there must have been challengers to overcome, but those challengers were handled in the family, not by the courts.

"Wow!" I heard a voice explode in the canyons of my thoughts.

Being brought back to where I was, I looked up to see a little boy standing with his tiny hand held by his dad looking in awe at the Lincoln Monument for his first time, his little frame balanced back on the heels of his shoes as his eyes turned skywards taking in the monument in all its gory.

"That's where President Abraham Lincoln is buried," I heard his father tell him, then listened to him tell his small son all about the President, and how someone who didn't like him, shot, and killed him.

"Shooting another person isn't right, is it daddy?" this little boy questioned.

I wondered if all little boys asked their father's that question after hearing the news about Abe Lincoln's Assassination. I wished they would have stayed there so I could hear more, but a woman towing another child walked up and together as a family continued their way to the entrance of Lincoln's Tomb.

Sitting there I started watching some of the groups that I had watched going in now come out. First thing I noticed was how quiet they had become, where before they had been talkative and laughing, they now walked to a different drum.

Again, I wished I had gone up and talked to them to get there retrospect on what they had newly learned from their visit to this great man's final resting place, but I didn't.

You might be asking yourselves, "why didn't I?" I knew I was going to write a book based around this trip. What better opportunity then now to get answers?

The answer is a simple one. I thought I'd be writing a completely different story, when in fact I didn't have a clue as to what turn would develop once I started writing.

Everyone coming out after their tour stopped and took photographs of the monument, standing there, with the afternoon sun giving it the same glow as earlier.

How quiet the entrance had become at this moment as the visitors exited, but the silence was short lives as loud voices coming from behind me ushered in another group of anxious students. Some wanting to learn, some just there for something different to do. Something signed-up for, but with little interest at the time.

They're in for a big surprise, I thought watching them gather.

I saw Ern and Big Bird exit and walk around behind the monument following the path laid out.

I knew there would be different conversation once we returned to the road, get on Route 66 which we had seen coming into Springfield, and continue our journey over Route 66 and to the St. Louis Arch better known as The Gateway Arch, and the next historic place on our trip.

CHAPTER 2

There wasn't much to see on Route 66 in Illinois until we drove into St Louis, Missouri, and spotted The St Louis Arch, which is also known as The Gateway Arch. Traffic was heavy, and no one really wanted to exit off and park to go on an arch tour.

Returning to 1968 in my mind, something I had done in the past every time I saw the arch, which I had on many occasions, I tried to remember any happenings there I and my traveling companion would have stopped at, and every time my mind draws a blank.

The only thing I remember the most was the highway cops weren't very friendly when it came to hitch hiking which probably stemmed from everything going on in Chicago concerning the Hippie movement and the gathering of protesters to the Viet Nam War.

If you are interested in learning more concerning The Gateway Arch you will have to go online or purchase one of the many picture story books about it.

It was at this time traveling this section of Route 66 where I started to witness the death of many of the small towns which were affected when Highway 40 was made, and went around them. No longer were they passed thru giving businesses the sales needed to stay alive. The town's streets were now empty. Lively businesses were now boarded up or caved in shells of once was.

Is that empty burger joint one where I had enjoyed a burger, fries, and a chocolate shake at, having earned enough money from pumping gas at the closed station across the street from it? My mind questioned.

I could only wonder.

Soon it was time to stop for the night. A Super 8, or Hotel 6 was our choice for the evening, along with some Taco's.

Next morning with Ern behind the wheel munching his McDonald's biscuit's with Strawberry Jelly, our journey continued. It was much like the previous day had been as far as Route 66 was concerned.

Gone quickly now was the desire to exit off the highway to follow the original Route 66. We knew there would be nothing to see, just more dead or dying towns where once lively ones had stood, flourished, and had given life to the 60's and to a couple long haired, hippie freaks just passing thru.

Crossing into Kansas we did choose to get on Route 66 to go visit the only surviving curved arch bridge on the entire length of the famous Mother Road, this being the Rainbow Curved Bridge which spans over the Brush Creek in Riverton, Kanas.

At first, the bright white of this newly painted landmark sparked a memory from a time long passed, and quickly died out as I realized there was no memory of this bridge at all. Knowing this to be a fact, I did walk around the bridge with my friends. The day was hot, and stifling, and soon beads of sweat covered my face. Walking to the bridge's end, I gazed down into the muddy colored water and wondered if years ago I might have been floating in that muddy water on an inner-tube with a joint in my mouth, and most likely a cold beer in my hand.

It seemed to me now, wherever there was water, there were many tubers enjoying the coolness offered up to them. Although not old enough to buy beer, there was always someone who was. Today, the water was void of any tubers, or for that matter, any life form at all.

I need to add some information here just in case you are confused concerning my hitching Route 66, and the Cadillac ride I had and write about.

Dave and I would hitch Route 66 many times in part in the future before our hitching days ended, and re-reading this story there is this confusion, along with the fact I couldn't remember the exact order some things occurred in.

Scanning the creeks bank, I didn't see where there had been any signs of life on them. I envisioned the banks lined with tubes left there for the next outing as they would have been years ago.

Staring into the still water, I tried with all of me to bring up memories from the past regarding this place, but could not even knowing I most certainly had.

Had I not swum here? I questioned myself. *Laid on its banks and smoked dope? Drank a cold beer? Took a trippppppp? But, try as I might, I just couldn't remember this place.*

Because there was so much happening all over the country during this time frame, we had chosen not to do any night travel, and would stop when it started to get dark.

The top ledge of an overpass bridge offered the greatest security, and sheltered place to spend nights. You were off the ground, sheltered from the elements, and most important, out of sight.

Focusing my attention back to the present, I watched my friends walk around taking pictures, and wondered what they were thinking. They read the historic plaque containing the bridges history, but that is all they could walk away with, they hadn't lived the 60's and experienced the happenings of the day, and what might be going on around this bridge. After all, it wasn't an historic bridge back then.

I knew Ern wanted to experience the simpler time in life the sixties offered. Was he hoping to maybe feel that here? Ern, like me, had worked all his life in different states, and at one time was living in the next state north of me only a couple hours' drive away.

He was married, has a bunch of step-kids, and for the most part, had never had the luxury of just sitting back with nothing to do except breath, and to go do whatever his mind, and body wanted to do. This was his time to do just that.

But that was the road he chose to travel down, where I on the other hand had chosen a different split in the road.

My road led me to experience the sixties to the max, and to the max I did. Because of this it would be very hard, and time consuming for me to come back into reality once it was over.

I think about the girl, whom to this day I think about at times who started the transformation from hippie to a more normal person, along with a shave and a haircut, I would enter the more normal world. An older girlfriend who would come back into my life, and who I would marry, have three sons, and divorce, and then my present wife who had to except those times my mind would become clouded over with the sixties, and the free spirit would enter my body, and mind for a spell, and cause all kinds of heck.

Even though those two roads were completely different, and lead in many different directions, they had joined up here on this trip, at this time in space. I was being shown something, and I needed to figure out what that something was, because maybe this was the direction my new book would take.

Erns, Big Birds, and my road would separate again once this trip was over, but we would know the way to travel if ever we wanted to visit, but I know we will stay in touch.

Our high school 50th Class Reunion is this year and we already plan on attending it, so we will see each other there along with classmates I haven't seen since graduation day. Many classmates have gone on. Some live far away and can't attend.

Knowing that neither of them had experienced the 60's as I had, I could only venture a guess as to what either of them were thinking as they walked around on this sixties landmark, with its new bright white coat of paint, probably covering over years of colorful graffiti. I smiled at the thought of peeling off the layers of paint to see the different transformations the bridge had gone through over the course of time. I envisioned large PEACE signs painted on the bridges end caps along with the colorful green leaves and the number thirteen.

I wondered if it ever carried the weight of demonstrators opposing the Vietnam War, or troupe carriers of soldiers from the local armory headed out to the Jolly Green Jungles of Vietnam, having to call in law enforcement to remove demonstrators who had joined hand and hand, and closed the bridge.

Whammmmmmm! A new realization hit me as these thoughts played around inside my head.

Up to this moment, I had always thought there was only the one thing that I hadn't experienced in the sixties, that being Woodstock, but now I realized I had never taken part in an Anti-War Demonstration. I guess because of my family's military background and the fact I had lost best friends, and had others over there fighting, I just couldn't do something like that which would in my eyes dis-honor them. I wanted a military career but had two parents disabled and being the only son had a high lotto number, and a 4-A class deferent.

A regret? Maybe. But one I don't think about other than at times like these.

These thoughts could only be had by someone like me who had experienced the full impact the sixties had on a whole generation.

"Hey Ern," I heard my voice shatter the quietness. "Have you ever floated down a river on an inner tube?"

I really didn't know what he or Big Bird would answer as we had went our separate ways once school was over and military obligations were satisfied. After my California venture, and crossing the country hitch hiking days were over, I had gotten married and moved out of state never to return except for short visits.

I watched Ern walk over next to me and turn to look over the bridges railing into the still, muddy water. For the first time on this trip, and another first, I realized I could have been in conversation with Chief.

Chief was the name we all called his dad, even his kids did. Ern's mom was called Wally! Another story!!!

"You look just like Chief," I blurted out.

"I've been told that," came his reply. "In answer to your question, Elmer. No I haven't."

Elmer. One of a couple of people to call me by my given name. Now remembering his whole family referred to me as Elmer. My family often called me Elmer also. *Simple enough answer,* I thought. Ern here again was just like his dad.

Never say more than you have to, Elmer, I could hear Chief tell me standing in the middle of their driveway, or in their barn looking over the antiques for sale.

For that moment, Ern was Chief, and a smile crossed my face, and then my lips turned downward as memory took over and told me that he to, just as the sixties, had PASSED AWAY!

The bridge was on a turn-off from the highway so that it could be visited. No other traffic interrupted our visit that day. I walked across the bridge as I probably had back fifty years ago, then, jumping into the driver's seat of the vehicle proceeded to drive across it to the cheers of Ern, and Big Bird.

Why did this seem like some big thing, I don't know, maybe because we all were, as this bridge was, still standing fifty years later?

The difference between that bridge and ourselves, even though we were still standing, was, the bridge sported a new, fresh coat of paint making it appear as if it was built yesterday, where our bodies had taken on the gift of time, aged, and had long ago forgone some of the things we had enjoyed when we were first built. HAIR, being one of them. Hahaha.

All in all we spent about one hour there at the Curved Bridge. Pictures taken that day would now have to last our lifetime knowing we would probably never travel this way again. I traveled across that bridge fifty years ago, and my life was changed forever. How different my life had been from Ern's and Big Bird's, but now, standing there with them both, and looking at our lives as they are today, I came to see they really weren't much different.

We had been married, divorced, re-married, kids, and grand-kids, and all three of us now retired, and standing in the heat of the day, on a bridge having ties to an era long passed, but looking for a moment to experience how it had been back then. All three of us, searching for a free feeling to get away from all the turmoil of today.

The sixties had their problems too. Assassination of a President, and other public figures such as Dr. Martin Luther King Jr., Robert Kennedy, Meager Evens, Malcolm X. We had riots in the streets, school shootings, etc. but through it all there was just a different feeling in the air.

There's some sadness seeing something you know will be for the last time, such as a bridge! Or a decade!

As we drove away that day, I watched Big Bird turn and watched as the brightness of the bridge disappeared from the rear window. My eyes turning to Ern who sat behind the wheel, he too, had his eyes in the rear view mirror watching its bright white structure fade out of sight.

See ya! Rainbow Curved Bridge, I whispered in my mind, turning at the last possible minute so I to could get a glimpse of it before it would be gone forever.

Once out of sight our trip continued, with the aggravating voice coming from the Tom-Tom on the dashboard.

"Make a U-Turn when possible!"

CHAPTER 3

"What's next?" the question was asked, ignoring the "make a U-TURN when possible" voice coming from the dashboard. Knowing the next state on Route 66 we would cross into was Oklahoma, I wanted to drive around the city and look up Big Chief and the other members of the 409 as seen on TV's Street Outlaws, but that wasn't going to happen, so it would be the Arcadia Round Barn located right on Route 66 in Arcadia, Oklahoma.

I will give you some quick facts concerning this historic landmark, and for closer details go and google it. There are tons of pictures on-line as well as facts written about it. The Arcadia Round Barn was built in 1898 by a local farmer. It was such a grand structure for its time that a second level was added as a community center for the town in 1920. The roof collapsed in 1988, and a full restoration was completed in 1992. It quickly became the most photographed sight on Route 66, and today is a gift center for Route 66 memorabilia along with other gifts.

Our visit there was on a day hot, and muggy. The barn lacked air conditioning, but had many fans running which made the place livable. As we walked around inside looking at the many framed pictures hanging on the walls which told of the barns history, I tried to look back to the year 1968 and imagine myself here, but had no recollection of it.

Just because you can't remember it now doesn't mean anything, I told myself. After all it had been fifty years since I had last set my eyes on this round barn.

Back in 1968 I wouldn't have been drawn to this barn anyways unless it was filled with my kind of people. Long-haired hippie freak sorts. I put my mind at rest, and just spent time walking around the inside admiring the great building feat it must have been when first constructed. Many of my earlier jobs had been in the construction field, and I'll tell you out straight, there would be no way I would have even come up with the design for a round barn, much less attempt to build one.

I learned that the second floor which acted as the town's community center now catered to all kinds of functions, such as weddings, and all sorts of parties, and it's huge, holds up to 150 people.

Forty-five minutes later, and armed with small bags of gifts, we were once again on the road. More run-down towns lay ahead as we listened to the aggravating voice coming out of the Tom-Tom, giving us directions to the Route 66 Historical Museum located in Elk City, Oklahoma. Being late in the day, the museum was closed so we found a room for the night close by, ordered pizza, and called it a day.

I left my room, and walked down to the corner of the lot where I could gaze up, and down the street. Looking to my left, and the part of the town that was most crowded with buildings, I could put myself amongst them, wash bucket in hand as I sat about washing some of their windows for food. Even though I couldn't really remember details of that time, I knew in my mind I would have been here doing just that! Washing windows or pumping gas.

There were some newer establishments such as the hotel we were staying at which wasn't here back in 1968. Small one pump gas stations, and corner markets had long closed and were now run-down shells giving way to the eight pump convenient market all-in-one just off the entrance to the interstate.

Opening the door to my room, I was hit by a blast of frigid air. My face, arms, and hands were covered with sweat from the short walk back to my room in the ninety plus temperature.

Packing in the morning, and after driving through McDonalds for Ern's two biscuits with strawberry jelly, we made our way back to the Route 66 Museum.

What a good time walking through the displays and out buildings. Along with their displays of Route 66 nostalgia and memorabilia products, I enjoyed the old blacksmith shop the best, and spent about half an hour there in conversation with the old blacksmith volunteer. He showed great interest hearing about our trip along Route 66 in celebration to my fifty year old one back in 1968.

Back in the gift shop, talking with the cashier, I exchanged a signed copy of my book Between the White Line and the Fence Post for a lapel pin from the museum.

The book, *Between the White Line and the Fence Post,* referring to my 1968 journey down Route 66. I just received an email from her stating they were interested in stocking this book in their gift shop.

From here all the way to Barstow, California was very familiar to me. I had traveled this route many time when the job called for me to do so. I would have liked to have ventured off to go visit some of the western towns I had visited in the past, and write about in my western novels, but they were a drive from where we were, but we were planning a side-trip to go to Tombstone.

From the Historical Museum we returned for a short drive on Route 66 before returning to Route 40, and crossing Oklahoma, and into the state of Texas.

For those of you readers who have never driven through the Panhandle of Texas, trust me when I say, you haven't missed a thing.

Here in the town of Shamrock, we stopped for a visit to a restored Conoco filling station which was now a museum, gift shop. There was a Coffee Café there, but it was closed. Being the only ones there that day, we spent time looking at all of the memorabilia for sale along with your typical Route 66 gifts. Here I gave the counter woman a signed copy of my book, *Between the White*

Line and the Fence Post, in exchange I received a tee shirt.

Here, as my traveling companion shopped around inside, I went out into the hotness of the day you can only experience in the Texas Panhandle. I reached out with sweaty hand and ran it over the restored gas pump stopping at the shiny pump handle.

Could I have held this pump in my hand fifty years ago, I asked myself? Trying hard to create some sort of a vision of a long hared, hippie just wanting to earn a couple of dollars for a burger and fries.

I looked up and down the street as if looking for the next auto to pull in for gas, but there would be no one today. Here again the station was only an un-working station from a decade which passed into obscurity many years ago.

Its in-ground holding tanks now either removed of filled up with sand. Never again to hold the fuel to power present day autos passing through.

The gas stations of today all being self-serving wouldn't have allowed me a chance to earn the money needed for food, so I could continue on with my trek back then. Ern, and Big Bird along with so many others didn't, and would never experience pumping gas to earn a few dollars for burger, fries, and chocolate shake.

How many of you readers had after school jobs, week-end jobs, pumping gas? Many of you did, I'm sure of that statement.

While in school I worked at FRANK'S TEXACO STATION, pumping gas a trade that would be of assistance once I hit the road.

Shamrock had become another causality caused when Route 66 was decommissioned, and Route 40 was built. In it prime hay day, Shamrock would grow in population to over 3,700. Today that number is below 1,900.

The heat was quickly catching up to me, so I went back inside and enjoyed an ice cold Coke before we said our good-byes.

"Did you pump gas here, Elmer?" the voice of Big Bird asked.

"Couldn't tell you for sure, but probably did," I answered him while watching the station slowly shrink out of sight.

"Probably pumped gas, smoked some weed, had a few cold beers, and messed around with one of the local hippie girls who always seemed to locate me whenever we would enter a town," I exclaimed. "Who knows? Could have been that lady we just visited with," I laughed out-loud while saying it.

As funny as a long shot as that might seem, it might just have been.

Towns were small, and word would move about quickly informing everyone some hippies were in town, for not all of the country embraced the Hippie Movement, for some it was just the opposite as we would find out while making our way across the Panhandle.

An attraction that wasn't on Route 66 in the Panhandle back in 1968 was a place that has come to be known as The Cadillac Ranch. Cadillac Ranch is located just a couple of miles west of Amarillo, Texas and is the name given to a section of farm land where ten pointed finned 1960's styled Cadillac's lay half-buried, nose down in the dirt. Cadillac Ranch was the brain-child idea of two San Francisco Architects and an art student, so Cadillac Ranch became a part of what was known as the Ant Farm Project.

You can do a web search for the Cadillac Ranch and get all the information on it and the whole idea behind its creation, and plus there are hundreds of photos of the psychedelic painted cars sticking out of the ground their surface coated many times over with all the colors of the rainbow

As we drew nearer to the ranch you can see it off in the distance, and you can't really make out exactly what you are looking at because of the distance it is from the road. It's not until you get opposite it that you get a clear picture of it, even then, you wonder just what you're looking at.

You see there's a front street, which on the day we were there was lined with cars, and all around the display of buried Cadillac's was a throng of individuals with cans of spray paint. All would-be artist waiting their turn to paint their initials on the surface of a Cadillac, take their picture so they could show family, and friends back home they had visited the Historic Cadillac Ranch.

So here we were about to join in. Ern had brought his own cans of spray paint for home. His and his wife's initials would even be painted on with paint from his home state of Tennessee. I wondered if she picked out the colors. Spray painting graffiti, pictures, designs, and your initials on the cars surfaces has been going on since the conception of the Cadillac Ranch.

I questioned in my mind if that was what the inventors of the Cadillac Ranch had intended?

Over time, layer, upon layer of spray paint has distorted the original lines of the Cadillacs. The Cadillac's are located quiet a distance from the parking area, and it became a struggle for me to make the walk. Plus there was what seemed like a twenty mile-an-hour head wind blowing up dust like crazy, but I made the walk slowly following my two friends.

It didn't take me too long to realize I should have left my hat in the vehicle.

That twenty mile-an-hour headwind was threatening to remove it, and claim it for its own. My right hand held tightly over it wasn't going to let that happen.

There were people everywhere and Ern had to wait a few minutes as someone completed their task of painting what was a large PEACE SIGN on the trunk of one of the Cadillacs.

There it was! My mind exploded! Instantly I was transported back to the 60's and the happenings going on during that time period. It was while I was standing there I remembered, with a big smile on my face, the very day on a much needed trip to Boston where I stood in front of a tattoo parlor contemplating getting a large PEACE SIGN tattooed on my back, but I didn't. It amazes me now why I never got a tattoo, and I secretly thought of getting a Route 66 one to always remember this trip by, but again I didn't

Many to this day who grew up in the 60's think the Peace Sign was the brain-child of some pot-smoking-anti-war-hippie, but it wasn't. The Peace Sign was designed overseas in direct opposition to Nuclear Testing. The interior of the circle was formed by the flag signal for the letter "N" and the letter "D" in reference to Nuclear Disarmament. It was brought to the United States in 1958 where during the Vietnam War era it quickly became an Icon in direct opposition to the war. You don't see it displayed as such today, even though there are conflicts going on here and abroad.

In the 60's if you had a VW Van or such, you had a large PEACE SIGN painted on it along with all the graffiti, just like I was witnessing here as this kid finished his interruption of the beloved PEACE SIGN over the brightly colored trunk section of a Cadillac.

"Oh crap!" I screamed, as my right hand lacked its grip on my hat, and it was instantly claimed by the ever blowing wind. I sure wasn't worth running after as it was gone before it hit the ground. Me and several others watched as my custom made Brad Paisley look-a-like hat sporting a custom made beaded hat band made by a friend in Colorado, high-tailed it across the wheat field. I thought I would feel some sort of loss not only for the hat, but what it had cost, but I didn't.

This trip had made me realize when something that was is no longer there, it is no longer there, and as much as you want the past to continue, and not change, it does. And when it changes you can't bring it back, such as all those torn down gas stations, or shells of them. Empty for years, now in so bad of shape one couldn't bring it back to life it they wanted to.

"Oh well," was all I could think of to say, then continued with, "The answer, my friend, is blowing in the wind, the answer is blowing in the wind."

Ern finally sat his spray can down and indicated he was satisfied with his results, and now it was time for a final snap-shot.

I recall with a film camera you took only one shot because film was expensive to buy and develop, but today with our digital phone cameras, and cameras, we tend to take many if not hundreds. Which reminds me, I just received a package from Ern with all the stuff I left in the vehicle. Along with the stuff was a jump drive with 1,400 pictures and 7 videos of our trip.

See what I'm talking about.

Returning to the vehicle, we were blocked in, so we had to go down the road a piece to turn around. GOOD THING! There, caught in the chain link fence was my hat. Dangling down next to it, also caught by a barb on the fence, was my custom hat band. Just like some of the restored building, and bridges from our past that have refused to die, so had my hat.

CHAPTER 4

"Bet you never thought you'd see that hat again, did you Elmer?" Asked Big Bird with a loud laugh.

"No, for sure. I thought it was gone forever just like these old buildings and ghost towns we've been passing through," I replied.

My putting the likenesses between the two happenings were starting to set the tone for this trip. It was what we call and refer to as *The Cycle of Life*. We are born, we live a given number of years, and we die. Our Cycle of Life holds true for anything. Rather it be something that is alive with flesh and blood, or concrete, and wood.

I knew I was being shown something important, in regard to this trip, and my purpose for being on it other than just for nostalgia sake.

"Can you believe the hat band was there also? What were the chances of that happening?" I stated shaking my head in disbelief.

One hears about stories such as these every day, but when it happens to you it just brings everything into perspective.

Adrian, Texas was the next stop on the Route 66 guide, and a place called Mid-Point. Mid-Point is nothing more than a wide white line painted across the highway indicating this is the halfway point between Illinois and

Santa Monica, Ca. on Route 66. A diner there had the best ever chocolate shakes made before your eyes with real ice cream and cream. A slice of one of their ugly pies wasn't bad either. The diner here has changed hands many times over the years, but at least it is still original as it was back in the 60's.

More photos and we were back on the road again.

Over the years I have been at this one spot on numerous occasions, and people I have come in contact with have always asked that one question, "Why is Mid-Point such an important place to me?" I always try my best to answer in a way they can understand. Mid-Point to me is one of two locations in the whole United States that defines a location.

The other one is the Four Corner Monument where there is a plaque defining where four states have come together. Those four states are, Utah, Arizona, Colorado, and New Mexico.

Getting back to Mid-Point. Here is a wide line painted across the original Route 66 which was by-passed in 1969 by Interstate 40. I would bet there are hundreds of travelers passing by on the Interstate not even aware of this important part of history. Here, you can stand on the painted line, face the large sign and know you are 1,139 miles from end to end on Historic Route 66. 1,139 miles from Chicago, 1,139 miles from the Santa Monica Pier.

Just as standing on the Four Corner Monument with a foot in Utah, another foot in Arizona, bend down and place a hand in Colorado, and the other hand in New Mexico, the only place in the whole United States where four states have come together to form four corners.

This got me thinking. *I wonder if there was some location marked off as being the half-way point from East Coast to West Coast.*

Going to the ever knowledgeable Internet I quickly learned there was, and it was located in Kinsley, Kansas on Route 50. A large marker there stated it was the Mid-Point between East New York, and West San Francisco, 1,561 miles in either direction. I mentioned this to my traveling companions, and all I got was, "Really!" There was no desire to go stand there.

Why? I asked myself. *What was it about Mid-Point on Route 66 that made it more important than Mid-Point in Kansas?*

Stretching out in the back seat and listening to the two of them in conversation the answer came to me.

It was where it was located, that being on the Mother Road, Route 66, and, Route 66 was associated with the whole Hippie, Free Love Movement that defined the 60's. I knew Ern wanted to once again capture the free feelings the 60's had to offer.

But wait! My brain exclaimed. Ern and I graduated high school in 1968 and he had never shown an interest in the Hippie Movement and what it offered. He joined the service after school, shipped off to Vietnam, and when he returned it was the 70's, the 60's were over.

Here the answer came to me. Ern didn't want to go back and re-live the 60's, no, he wanted to experience them. Traveling Route 66 and going through its many museums, and seeing how some of these townsfolk still lived, he was in some small way hoping to see what a way of life was offered by the 60's. Although a pretty straight looking guy in school, I was truly imbedded in the movement from 1966 on to its end, and once the 60's were over! They were over.

As my eyes slowly closed, I knew I was onto something when I heard the words, "I wonder what it was like back then?"

I was right. They wanted to experience that what they had only read about.

Neither had never floated down a river on an inner tube, drinking a cold beer, or smoking a joint, or even tripping on a suburb hit of ACID not a worry in the world at that moment.

My book, *Between the White Line and the Fence Post,* touches on as to what Hippie Life was in the 60's if you wanted to embrace it. Coming to this realization I searched my mind laying there looking at the red sky through the window, what was it I was searching for? I lived the 60's once! I wouldn't want to go back and do it all over again, because I probably wouldn't change a thing. It wasn't until the early 70's after meeting a girl I'll refer to as MJ that I wanted to make the change.

There was no way to carry the 60's into the 70's if you were going to make anything of your life.

Was this time my Mid-Point in life?

Unlike the two Mid-Points I have mentioned, we don't know how long a life we will live here on earth so how could we put a line down that would define our Mid-Point in life?

Here my mind seemed to overload with questions. If the early 70's could be defined as the Mid-Point of my life, I wouldn't be here now. My life would have ended at the age of forty-six or around that age. I'm sixty-eight now so that couldn't be. This trip down memory lane really was for a purpose more than just going back and visiting the past for me anyways, or trying to determine what the Mid-Point was in my life.

No. It was to show me although you have a set date, and time marked down on your Birth Certificate as to the time your life started on earth, you will never see the end date so there really is no definite Mid-Point in one's life that you could paint a line at. If you could, than you would know when your life will come to an end, and there is only one person who knows that date. He is GOD ALMIGHTY.

I knew now the meaning of the Mid-Point markers in reference to distance traveled or going to be traveled has no bearing on how we live, or not live or life.

If we had the end date than it would, but we don't have that date, so we can't waste one precious minute worrying about that Mid-Point in our lives, trying to determine that Mid-Point in my life has taken up so much of my time lately, but it won't anymore. Wow! If a painted line across the road could open my eyes, and mind in this sort of way, than I couldn't wait to see what the rest of the trip would show me. All the thoughts and earlier notes I had jotted down to get an idea for a new book were now rendered useless.

"Tucumcari, New Mexico!" I heard Big Bird call out. Hotel room, food, bed all three sounded good after traveling all day.

One of my big worries on this trip was going to be my health. Besides having Parkinson's I had just gotten out of the hospital fighting off a bout with Pneumonia and it had been about seven years since I had last been on any kind of trip any further than the grocery store, or Wal-Mart, so I was somewhat concerned. I didn't want to spoil the trip for my friends by having to cut it short because of me. I do have some walking issues, but worked around them, and we all were able to see, and do that what we came on this trip to do.

After a good night's sleep, no one wanted a breakfast of Ostridge, so it was once again McDonalds, than off to the Route 66 Auto Museum located in Santa Rosa. Ern, and I had always been *GEAR HEADS,* so a visit to this museum was a must.

Inside we met Maria, whose sister Anna owned the place, and who would later trade me a signed copy of my book Between the White Line and the Fence Post for a tee shirt. Their cars were ok. There wasn't anything there that jumped up and said WOW, but what they had was a good collection, and they had three like cars that either Ern or I had owned. What I really enjoyed was all the other memorabilia on display. Here again old memories from the past came out. Some to put a smile on my face, some to draw a tear from the corner of my eye. I saw those same looks on the face of Ern, and knew in jest what he was remembering although his story-line might be somewhat different than mine.

After picture taking, we left Route 66, got on Route 54 to make our way down south where we could jump on Route 10, so we could go to Tombstone, Arizona, the only place I had told the guys I wanted to visit that was out of the way. I have been to Tombstone several time during my working days, and one I have included in some of my western writings.

I recall as a small boy sitting in front of a black-n-white TV screen watching a western called Tombstone Territory. "Whistle a tone that will carry me, to Tombstone Territory." But why was Tombstone more dear to me then let's say, Dodge City, or Abilene,

Kansas? Just to name a couple. We all witnessed gunfights in the street, enjoyed a burger and a Sarsaparilla in the Long Branch Saloon, and the show where actors re-enacted the Gunfight at the OK Correl. It was a good show, but hot, and sticky, and because of my medication, I had to find a cooler place. The show was over anyways.

My thoughts were what they have always been at times like these. *I was born in the wrong century, in the wrong state.*

Ern, and Big Bird went up, and down the street visiting all of the gift shops, and the only remaining establishment from Tombstone's hay day, The Bird Cage Theatre.

The Bird Cage Theatre was many things. It was a gambling hall where it was said the longest game in history was played. That game lasted over eight years and some of the players were, Doc Holiday, Diamond Jim Brady, and Bat Masterson.

It was also home to the wickedest brothel around which operated 24/7 from its conception in 1881 till it closed when the silver mines shut down in1892. The Bird Cage would be bought, and re-opened as a tourist attraction in 1934. Today you can visit the downstairs, and the back rooms, and the cribs where the prostitutes serviced the lonely cowboys who had the price.

Three fires and the flooded silver mines were what ended Tombstone. The Bird Cage was the only brick building, so it survived.

The next obvious stop was Tombstones famous Boot Hill Cemetery. All western towns had a Boot Hill Cemetery which was in reference to the many cowboys and gunfighters who were killed and buried there with their boots on.

Some young gunslinger, who after too much to drink thought himself bulletproof, and let his mouth get him into a gunfight. Blurred vision, unsteady hand, the outcome already known. No one knew who the young gunslinger was, so he would occupy one of the un-known headstones in the cemetery.

Here amongst the hotness of the day, walking with sweat running from my forehead, and into my eyes, setting them on fire due to the salty liquid, and regardless how my eyes squinted, they catch a familiar name on one of the markers. Frank McClaury, I know the name because I just watch the re-enactment of the Gunfight at the OK Corral. I than spy Billy Clanton, and Tom McClaury, others who met their maker on the Twenty-six day in October of 1881. Although there were eight participants at the gunfight, only these three were killed, and reside in Tombstone's Boot Hill.

I notice a trend as I walked about the many named, and un-named grave markers. Markers listing cause of death anything from drowning, killed by Indians, lynched, murdered, suicide, some shot by a jealous husband or wife. Not unlike walking through a present day cemetery were my thoughts.

One of the things I had enjoyed while traveling the country was visiting the many cemeteries I would pass. Some nicely kept, some overgrown with weeds and small trees. Named, and un-named headstones. Headstones baring cause of death. No different than those I was looking at here in Tombstone's Boot Hill.

Times change. Advances are made in medicines, and technologies. Advances in building materials, but life! Life doesn't change. We are born, live, die. The cycle of life, and it doesn't matter where you are born or year. No, nothing can change the cycle-of-life, and we don't know what our cycle-of-life will be.

CHAPTER 5

The WigWam Motel in Holbrook, Arizona, would be our home for the night. Ern had read about it with its old cars used as props around the parking lot, and its tie to Route 66 and the 60's.

The wigwams were made out of fiberglass or closed-cell spray foam. This place was in need of some up-dates. Everything was what it had probably looked like in 1950, when they were constructed, except for the flat screen TV and an air conditioner. No phone, or clock radio sat atop the very small bed stand. The WigWam Hotel was located right on Route 66. It was one of seven sights built all around 1950. Only three operate today, one in California, one in Kentucky, the others given ground for more modern hotels. Again, I'll refer to the *all-knowing Internet* for more information.

Over my writing years, I have done a lot of research for my novels, and I have come to love the Internet, and there isn't a writing day that goes by where I haven't opened up a google search engine searching for an answer to a question, or a desire to capture that one, right, word to add interest to my writing, so you the reader I keep your interest, and sparks a desire for you to read more.

An author once told me that a writer isn't so un-like a good artist. A good artist paints a picture so that you have a visual of what he has pictured in his mind, and he wants to share that picture with you. Being a writer, you have to paint that same picture, but with words, not paint. The authors I enjoy reading the most, have learned to do just that, and it's what I strive to do with my writings.

I did a web search on the WigWam Hotel. The many pictures there were from when it was first built. Let me tell you. They were bright white up-side-down "V's" reaching for the sky, adorned with red, yellow, and black characters of Indian design. I learned some very interesting facts concerning wigwams. Now to most they would say, who cares? When told these structures weren't really wigwams but tipis.

Wigwams were domed shape, and a tipi was coned shape just like the ones we were staying in. So why did the builders of this hotel name them Wigwams instead of tipi's? The TiPi Hotel would have sounded the same as the WigWam Hotel? He could have even misspelled it and written the TeePee Hotel. Now, lost forever is the answer to that question. But again, one would ask, who cares?

As we rounded the street corner to pull into the parking lot, and search out our wigwam number, Big Bird brought it to our attention that there was a hobo wandering around a broken down shed next to the railroad tracks off to the side of the WigWam Village we were staying at.

Ern stopped the vehicle, and we sat there and watched him as he continued walking around. He had a back pack which he carried in one hand, he had a tall walking stick in the other. Soon he disappeared from sight, and I knew he had found a way into the shed. This would be his safe place for the night. I envisioned him un-packing some of his private things and laying them out. If he was lucky, he might have a small McDonald's bag with a burger and maybe some fries.

I almost asked Ern let's go to the convenient store where I would buy him something to eat, and drink.

In my travels, I would see some of the less fortunate on the corners of the interstate, or entrance to truck stops, and I would go inside and buy some food for them. They always said the same thing when I handed the bag to them along with cold drinks. "Thank you, and GOD Bless."

This instance was different as he had already gone from site, and in his safe place, and you didn't want to bother him, this I learned from a couple transients I bought food for one day when I pulled into a Burger King and spotted them in the dumpster.

We sat and talked for about an hour. Me asking all kinds of living questions to them. It was from them I learned so much about their lives, and their routines.

Some of them really have money but choose to live this way, but most don't live this sort of life by choice, regardless to what a lot of folks think.

My thoughts went back to the year 1968. It could have easily have been me walking around outside of that shed looking for a way in, so I could have a safe place to spend the night. My mind slipped back to that fearful night in Texas where Dave, and I thought our lives would end, and our hitch hiking days after that were changed, and we looked for those safe places to spend the nights. I write about that in my book *Between the White Line and the Fence Post.*

It was for this reason I didn't mention anything to Ern, but just sat there in thought remembering, until he was gone from sight. Seeing him, like I stated brought back a ton of old memories, but before I had any more time to, memory surf, we pulled into the office area and time to go and get checked in. We learned of a restaurant/bar down the street that had good food, so once we dropped off our things and freshened up, off we went.

I had quit drinking in the year 2001, when I also quit smoking. After all, one can't have a cold beer without a smoke to go along with it, but the cold beer looked so good I came within an arms-reach of picking up a frosted mug sitting on our table.

Sitting next to our table was a woman and a younger guy, both had Margaritas in front of them along with shot glasses turned upside down on the table. It was obvious they were celebrating something because they kept toasting the air, and were very loud. The woman wasn't unlike a lot of women who have had enough to drink, or for that matter, a hippie girl back in 1968 who had, had enough to smoke!

I'll just refer to her as Pocahontas, a name given to her by Big Bird. It wasn't long before we knew her whole life's history. She was in the medical field, or something like that, and had just retired after thirty-one years. Broken-up with a guy who was a mommies-boy, and believe it or not, she was also going to write a book which sparked an interest in myself and I shared with her the fact I have written fifteen books.

Even these times hadn't changed over a fifty years span. A drink, or a joint, brought about conversation even though you didn't know the other person. I have had several lifelong friends which came about in this way, but those were the exceptions, most of the hundreds I partied with are nameless, faceless shells today, just as they were back then. Some of those who have walked into my existence have left life-long impressions on my life. You might not figure that out right away. Sometimes it might take you years to understand their importance in your life.

Today I have learned to pay attention to those who come into my life even if it is for a moment in time before they leave, and by their leaving you can definitely feel an emptiness their non-presence causes. You never know what future plans have been laid out there for us, but we have choices to make that affect them, so it is our walk in life to choose the best path to walk.

I tried walking that path on my own, and made lots of mistakes along the way, which is very typical for someone who was born in the 1950's and who choose the paths I had chosen in the 60's. I use the plural for path, because I choose many different ones because I had all the answers. Being a free spirit I tended to go off in different directions if an opportunity presented itself, and disregarded what the consequences might be for making the choices I would make.

I lived my life for that instant gratification.

Over the years I have paid the price for the paths I have walked, but that's okay, because it was the paths I chose. There have been many times I have said to myself, *only if I had chosen that path or this path,* but I can't go back and change anything. No, and neither can you go back and make changes to your life. Not one single thing.

Isn't or minds a fascinating instrument? All these thoughts running through it in the blinking of one's eye. Just like mine was doing now. All these thoughts and still attentive to pulling into the parking lot of WigWam Village.

We said goodnight, and as I headed to my wigwam I spied a soft orange glow coming through some large cracks in the old shed we watched a person go into earlier. Instantly, I was that person sitting in there, in my safe place watching the flames, slowly lower the lids of my eyes, and enjoying the smells, and crackling sounds the fire made. No matter how hot the evenings were, a fire always seemed to take away all of the days issues that might have arose.

Today, behind our home along with our sons, and daughters is a fire pit. As a matter of fact, just last night after supper at our daughters next door, my fourteen year old granddaughter Lauren made me my first S'more in god knows how long it's been!! It was hot and humid out, but there we all were, enjoying a roaring fire, making S'mores, and sitting quiet as the fire sang its evening song to comfort us, relax us, take away all of the days issues.

I would have liked to have gone and joined that hobo's fire, but couldn't. I needed to get where it was cooler, and my wigwam was freezing cold as I had turned the air down as low as it would go. Without even undressing, I flopped down on the bed, pulled the colorful Indian blanket over me, and closed my eyes to capture that fire the lone person was enjoying in the shed across from the tracks.

Tomorrow was going to be a big day of local sightseeing before driving up to the Grand Canyon, and then onto Santa Monica Pier, and the end of Route 66.

The night passed quickly, and before I knew it, it was 6:00am and I could hear Ern outside probably washing the windshield which he did every morning along with checking fluid levels, and tire pressure. He had a dash mounted video camera which he had on a lot. He would have a GREAT record of this trip that's for sure.

A loud knock on the door, and I knew I'd find Big Bird there when I opened it.

Big Bird sure was GOD's BLESSING to me on this trip. He seemed to know in advance what I needed, and he always had my cane ready, and a strong arm to help me in, and out of the vehicle, and if the hotel offered it: A coffee and breakfast, always a yogurt, and a spoon.

Big Bird didn't mind staying back when I couldn't keep up to Ern who always seemed on a mission when we got someplace of interest.

Bags packed away, we left the WigWam Village, made our way to McDonalds, then off to Holbrook, and the Petrified Forest. We were early, so we waited in the parking lot with several others, all making small talk saying where they were from, and where they were head.

A motorcycle group roared in. They were all older and from California and soon we were in conversation with them. Like us, they would do this tour then head up to the Grand Canyon. In conversation with the leader, I mentioned they needed to be sure to pass through Winslow, Arizona, and go STAND on the CORNER in WINSOW ARIZONA, a favorite tourist spot.

The ranger arrived and opened the gate and we all went our separate ways.

The drive through Petrified National Forest Park was beautiful. The colors were in creditable. Over the years I have passed this National Land Mark many times but never drove through it, now though, I sat on the edge of the seat taking it all in.

For those of you reading this book let me tell you first hand. "This all didn't just happen!" You feel a different kind of peace driving through the forest. Well, there really isn't a forest to speak of, just petrified trees laying in the earth, their bark, once alive with life now turned to stone.

There are many turn-offs so you can stop and get out of your car and gaze out over an area colored with many shades of reds, blacks, whites, and the such.

The beauty of what your eyes are taking in, over-rides the heat of the morning sun now adding its bright yellow haze out over the land adding to the color scheme.

My eyes turned to look at my traveling companions, and as I did, I noticed something, and that was the quietness of that morning. Not only was it so quiet standing here you could hear a pin drop, neither one of us had uttered a word since we drove through the main gate, and into the park. There was a peace here and it was easily felt. The vast land before your eyes undaunted with house and super-highways, noisy trucks, and trains, there wasn't even a loud-mouth bird calling out for a companion. No! None of the above, just a quietness that was all encompassing.

I had a side view of Ern's face and wondered if he was feeling what I was feeling, for if he was, I knew he was feeling that peace and freedom he was searching for out there on Route 66.

CHAPTER 6

There isn't any of Historic Route 66 through Arizona left it is paved oved by Route 40, but because the highway traveled across the plains and was the only road, I got the same feelings I must have had back when I traveled over this now newly paved highway Route 40.

Amazing how your memories can open up and reveal things from your past, for right now I was seating in the back seat of a 1966 Eldorado Cadillac, stoned on some Texas Red Bud, listening to an up and coming heavy rock band called Led Zeppelin whose sound was splitting the speakers behind my head.

At that time, I made a mental note concerning their sound. Theirs wasn't the Psychedelic sounds that I usually listened to, but a pounding sound that went to your very core, shook it up, and threatened to break every bone in your body. Later on in the early 70's the Who, Stones, and Black Sabbath would fill out my eight-track collection. The 70's would usher in a new era in time and along with it, new sounds.

It sometime amazes me where a song can conger up a specific year, and sometime a specific day. I don't recall a whole lot concerning that time way, way, back in 1968 only fleeing snap-shots, partly because we hitched a ride that brought us from New Mexico all the way to the end of Route 66 in California. He was towing a–Haul with a piece of equipment from Cleveland, Ohio to Barstow, California, but also, I would go on the road for another year crisscrossing the US, and traveling Route 66 many times.

Up until this very minute I had remembered that part of our trip back then as being good. We had snared a lift which would bring us all the way to California. Hurray! The driver had uppers, and downers, Dave, and I had LSD, and pot. What could be more right with our world? Then the Twin Arrows Truck Stop came into the picture.

The Twin Arrow Truck Stop had for its signage two telephone poles resembling arrows, donned with plywood feathers, and arrow heads, and stuck in the ground at an angle. They are still there. Re-furbished, and sticking up into the Arizona sky. Twin Arrow Truck Stop is a rundown place today as we would stop when we encountered it, but back then it was a hopping place in the middle of nowhere, Arizona. Take a few minutes and do a web search on Twin Arrow Truck Stop, you will find many interesting write-ups and pictures there.

The fond memories I had carried all these years now came back to me as not being so fond. Over the years I have passed here many times, stopping to check out the empty shells which used to make up a lively truck stop, trading post which finally succumbed to the times in 1995.

Today, I had Ern pull in and we all got out and walked around. Gone now were all signs of life. Twin Arrows was dead. Big Bird, and I stuck together as we wondered in, and out of the empty buildings, once alive with truckers, travelers, and the smells, and sounds, associated with a fast food diner.

It was here, and long ago lost to memory, Dave, and I encountered our second bout with hostility. The hostility I was remembering at this time came in the form of a young prostitute and two burly truck drivers. The girl left the table she was at containing the two truckers, and came over to our table where she took the empty seat next to our driver. Up close, she wasn't as young as she had looked. She told us she never had a long-haired hippie before, much less two.

Looking towards the driver, I saw him give a slight, no, shake of the head just as I was pulled from my seat by one of the truckers, Dave right behind me. Dragged through the door, and out into the parking lot both Dave, and myself started to feel the wrath these two truckers had for longhaired hippie people who they thought was a threat to stealing their GOOD-TIME for the evening. No one else followed us outside, not even our driver so this must have been a familiar happening. Why hadn't I remembered this? I could only venture a guess.

It has been my lot in life to overlook the bad and concentrate on the good, must be what happened here.

This encounter soon got bloody as both Dave, and myself, were armed with razor sharp switch-blades, and neither of us afraid to inflict pain of the cut if necessary.

I had an older brother who once told me if ever in a fight, make sure you mark-up the others face so that every time he looks in a mirror he remembers to never F&%# with you again. Instantly, two bright red lines crossed the trucker's face who had just grabbed my other arm. I knew what he was feeling. I had inflected these very cuts many times in the past knowing my sharp, pointed knife had cut deep, and inflected the max of pain.

Gone now was the hand which had grabbed my other arm. My swift kick in his neither region brought him to his knees where I swiftly kicked him in the face, breaking several of his front teeth.

Looking over towards Dave, I saw he had the same effect on the trucker who had dragged him from the diner. His bloody face resembled my trucker who was spitting blood out of his mouth. If it wouldn't have been for our stop here this day, this memory would have been lost forever.

Looking around now, I even found the very spot the encounter had taken place at. As stated earlier. Our minds are something great which we all have to understand, and search our memories often to unlock its past. I wondered what other memories this trip might unlock. I was almost afraid to find out, but at the same time excited, because here was a side of my 1968 trip I had long forgotten.

Already this trip had turned into a bitter sweet on as old memories thought to have been happy one were exposed as not to be exactly how my memories had recalled them to be. Although I have been in many a knife fight, my face bares no scars, but my hands and arms tell a different story.

The story begins at the Weirs Beach Drive-In Movie Theater, and by a knife yielding young lady named Terie. To add to the flare of my 1968 road trip, I'll tell you this story concerning Terie.

It was a different time, the year 1972. Gone from me and my way of life were the 1960's, although still loving LSD, and some of the other drugs which had made their appearance into the 1970's or the "ME decade" as novelist Tom Wolfe titled it. It seemed the whole planet was in turmoil, either man-made or natural.

I had returned from my hitch-hiking journeys, and had started hanging out on the board-walk at the Weirs Beach with a crowd of teen-ages from Massachusetts.

Between a job, and drug money, I was a happy camper, driving the car of my choosing, and being looked-upon with envy.

I've always believed that one could classify himself rich if he was driving the car of his choosing, and that was me, now on with the story. As stated, I met Terie at the Weirs Drive-In Movie Theater. Me and friends hung out, down front, on the picnic tables that were set up for walk-ins and others. This night we found a group had taken over our table, they were all girls, and of course I told them they needed to leave our table and park their butts on one of the other tables.

You might think this petty, my table, but to me it was principle. Anyways this one girl, and the obvious leader of the pack, challenged me with the harsh words, "Make us."

As I stepped toward her, she whips out an out-the-front Stiletto knife with precision. I was surprised by this, and as I remember asked her if she really wanted to do what she had obviously intended. Usually, if my blade came out, the first thing I did, and one that caught the other off guard, was to inflict matching crisscrossed lines on either cheek, but I didn't, instead I just drought my blade out.

Why I didn't cut her I don't know, but my stalling allowed her to make a couple lightning strikes across my hands, and arm. To this day I bare those scars.

I recall saying something like, "You cut me!"

"Yes I did, didn't I?" She replied. "My name is Terie."

I went out with her for a couple of years till she graduated high school in Franklin. She had been sent there to live with her aunt and uncle. She was from Massachusetts and had started hanging out with a tough group, so her parents sent her away.

"Hey Ern. Remember a girl I went out with named Terie?" I hollered over to him from the broken down door way of what used to be the front door of the café.

"Yes I do. Whatever happened to her?"

"After she graduated, she went back home to where she came from. She asked me to go with her, but I didn't. Hey! Maybe I'll try to locate her through social media."

"What made you think about her?" asked Ern walking up to me.

"I was just standing here remembering something that happened to me fifty years ago, right here in this spot." Over the next few minutes I replayed for him the story about the truckers.

Big Bird came over. "Whatcha' all talking about?" he asked.

"Elmer here was just telling me an interesting story in regards to this place," Ern told him.

"Let's hear it Elmer." Big Bird said. He stood there and folded his arms across his chest and waited.

I continued the story, but now remembering more too tell. How the Cadillac driver had run out and was waiting for us with car running. How over the next hundred miles or so every truck we passed seemed to want the whole road and made it difficult for us to get by them. Three of four actually ran us off the road, but our driver was a pro, and he yelled loudly and gave the trucker the finger when we did make it past.

Ern, and Big Bird laughed.

"I've heard your traveling stories when you related them to Wally and have never heard that one, Elmer," echoed Ern, and Big Bird.

I was stunned at these memories.

"That's because I just now remembered it," I told him.

Have you ever remembered something that had happened in your life only to find out years later it didn't happen exactly as you thought you remembered it? Well! For me here it was.

I become speechless. My eyes clouded over with a salty liquid which burned like heck. Telling the story out-loud painted a different picture for me that day. I stood there in the middle of an overgrown lot which once was a truck stop parking lot, and just turned around slowly taking it all in.

The picture was different now. Over the years in my travels, I have passed Twin Arrows many times with fond memories of that trip of 1968 in my mind, but today that canvas and the picture I had painted on it was different then it truly was. A forgery sort of telling.

It was a slow walk back to the vehicle for me that day. The thought in my mind as we pulled back onto Route 40 was the title of my first wester novel A NEW DAWN at

TWIN ARROWS. To me, it was clearly a NEW DAWN, and it didn't matter if it was 1968 or 2018. My eyes were being opened as if for the first time awakening from a very long fifty year sleep.

CHAPTER 7

One of the biggest let down on this trip and one I have never seen although it did exist back in 1968 was Impact Crater also known as the Canyon Diablo Crater.

When we passed by here in 1968, it could have been in the dark of night, or we just chose not to stop because our ride wasn't going to.

I have seen many pictures on the web picturing Impact Crater and was looking forward to seeing it firsthand. Here again was a place I have passed by many times but have never stopped. I should have done my homework in regards to this location, for if I had we would have saved a lot of time not making the drive out to it.

"If I was to tell you something was *privately owned*, what vision would come to mind? Don't know? How do $$$$ signs grab ya?"

Driving up to the crater you can see why it is called an Impact Crater. It looks like a small mountain with the peak gone, sorta like a volcano. Pulling into the parking lot which on this day was packed we were excited just like others we saw exit their cars and head for the visitors center. Inside, my take on being privately owned proved correct. There was an $18.00 per person fee to get in.

There was a service booth there where you could leave your take on your crater experience. Several voiced their regards on finding out the fee, so of course we stood in the service line to voice ours also.

Standing there looking down at a check off sheet of paper the service person had on the desk in front of her, it became plain to see we weren't alone. I read entrance fee column box checked off the most. You would think people would quit supporting this site for if they did this price would change overnight. The visitor's center there must have cost millions, so let's not pay for it.

Soon the crater was forgotten as we exited off Route 40 and took Route 66 into WINSLOW, ARIZONA. Not much remembered here from 1968. Winslow didn't become a household name till referenced in the Eagles/Jackson Browne song of 1972 titled *TAKE IT EASY*. Today there is a statue on the corner where there is a small park and shops where tourist stop to take pictures. We, of course, were just like them, and waited our turn to get a picture. Familiar faces.

The motor cyclist we had meet at the Petrified Forest were there waiting their turn for pictures. We spied each other and it was like a family reunion.

What made this place so special? I questioned myself. For it truly was just that.

Was it the fact we were standing in a place we all had heard about from A SONG? Was it a continuation of our trip? Was it meeting back up with strangers we had meet many miles from here and had told them about this very spot we now stood on?

Questions, questions, questions, zigzagging across the canyons of my mind looking for answers but none would come.

I posted a picture on Face Book and got many responses of, *been there done that. Been there, done that. But why*? I asked myself, reading those responses. I came to the conclusion it was sorta like visiting Lincoln's tomb at the start of this journey, or why we watch programs, and pick-up the Rag Mags who write and give us all the goings on of the stars.

The question I would ask of all you readers concerning the stars is; Do you read the stories and put yourself in their shoes? Walking the life as a millionaire buying whatever makes you happy at the time? Do you read to watch them fall from the sky? Bodies broken. Minds now wasted by alcohol or drugs. Whose marriage has crashed, and burned?

My take on the stars is this. They are human just like you, and I. They are born, will live, and will die, just like you and me. They will need nourishment, and oxygen to breath. The difference being, they are always in the lime-light, so we know about their every little move.

I truly don't believe the stars get excited reading about their personal lives in the mags and on TV. That's the price they have decided they were willing to pay for the careers they choose. Drugs, booze, and sex, that's what the public wants to read about concerning them. You read very little about the more wholesome actors and sports figures.

So, how does this relate to bringing a group of old motorcyclist, and three over 60 travelers to be, standing on the Corner in Winslow, Arizona? I thought I had the answer but now nor so sure. I guess I'll store all this to memory and wait and see what the rest of the trip reveals.

This trip down memory lane and into the past sure was developing some new twist and turns, but the truth of the matter being, I wanted whatever memories that were needing to get out and wag their tail to get out and do just that.

We stayed in another hotel that night. For me sleep came quickly only this time when sleep came, and the dreams began, I was floating on a makeshift raft down the Mississippi River. Tom Sawyer, and Huck Finn called this their River Journey, so I will do the same seeing my dream started out as such.

Our River Journey of 1968 was one I have always remembered being one of the high-lights of our trip. Dave and I often spoke of coming back and rafting the full length of it all the way to the Gulf of Mexico, along with the Colorado River, but we never did, for once this trip was over, we would go our separate ways never to see each other again. How sad I thought now. Not only did we do all these things in 1968, but we would also spend another year traveling to all the other places we heard about where hippies were still going strong, but never indulged in another River Journey.

Exactly how we got to the Mississippi River I don't recall, but we were there with a bunch of other hippie's just lounging about, smoking, drinking, and listening to music when Dave and I got the idea to take some inner tubes and some old signs laying on the river bank and construct a raft, and float down the Mississippi River for a spell. We ended up doing just that. With the help of the guys, we soon had a pretty nice raft built, and were pushed out into the moving Mississippi River. The raft had a tarp draped over a 2x4 which acted as sun-block, and cover if it rained.

Whenever we saw an old farm or dock in the distance, and could get to it, we usually added to our bounty. We had cooking pots & pans, dishes, knives & forks, fishing poles, a tackle box filled with old rusty lures.

At one stop we found some bricks and constructed a fire pit. Many a hot dog was cooked over a fire in that pit. Many a joint lit from the fire off a small twig laid in its coal just for that purpose.

Nothing but fond, happy memories, or so I have come to remember them to be, and including them in my novel Between the White Line and the Fence Post.

But this dream took me down another path.

Dave and I saw the six men on shore get into their motor-boats and head in our direction. Up till now we had nothing but good times, so we didn't expect anything different here, but we considered ourselves more than capable of taking care of ourselves, and weren't naive to possible trouble.

The six men turned out to be younger than they had appeared. As they drew nearer, we could see they carried ball bats, not a very good sign. We both had knives and knew how to use them but against six guys with bats the outcome couldn't turn out good in our favor.

"Give them what they want, and don't pull your knife," Dave said in a low voice.

Three of them boarded our raft, tore through our back packs, taking our pot, and the few hits of LSD I had in mine. They beat us up, tore our raft apart, and left us floating in the river. I didn't know if there were gators here or not, so it didn't take me long to swim to shore.

Why hadn't I remembered this before? And why now?

My dream took me next to the Panhandle of Texas. My memories had always been quiet clear in regards to what happened here, so why the need now to relive it? My dream started out just like I always have told it, and ended the same. Nothing had changed, so why replay it again?

A loud knock on my door, and it was morning, and time to hit the road but not before the drive-thru at McDonalds.

Big Bird had made breakfast for him and me at the hotel, so armed with two biscuits with Strawberry jam from McDonald's, we were off to the Grand Canyon.

On the way out of town on a section of Route 66 were more empty gas stations, now just shells, and the ever present reminder that the past was no more.

Like in other towns along the Historic Mother Road, some of these stations although closed, had tried to survive, but without business, of course they couldn't. Sorta like the human being. Without food and water we can't survive either. It was pretty plain to see, and understand the reference they carried to my window into the past. It was a sad part of this trip for me.

I have traveled this section of Route 66 many times in the past for business and had seen this picture many times before. The difference this time being one of letting go. I didn't understand until now what that really meant.

Looking closely at these empty buildings it was obvious they were beyond repair, even if someone had the desire to re-open one of them, it would have to be torn down, and re-built all a new. Burying the past, birth to the new. All I was being shown was all black, and white to me.

As close as I had been to the Grand Canyon in the past, I had only been to it once and was looking forward to seeing it with my two high school friends. Ern I learned had ben to the canyon before, Big Bird hadn't so at least for one of us it would be seeing something truly awesome for the first time. Even for Ern, and myself, this visit to the canyon would be truly awesome for us to.

The tour buses for the canyon are color coded indicating where their tour goes so you can purchase your ticket according to what part of the canyon you wanted to visit. I didn't feel like I could get off, get on the tour bus, so Big Bird and Ern headed out on one of the tours, and I stayed behind and relaxed in one of the gift shops till they returned.

The parking lots were packed with cars, and buses, and laughing families were everywhere to see, young, and old.

Knowing the approximate time of the buses return, I was outside waiting for them when they got back, and was planning on them getting on another tour bus, but instead, Ern went to the ticketing office, while Big Bird came over to me. He told me while on the bus, they had learned if you were a Vet and had purchased a life-long parks pass, than you got to go to all the area's the park rangers had access to.

All those locked gates with combination locks would now give way to Ern's fingertip, and give us a view of the canyon few ever have the opportunity of seeing, and it was truly majestic. Gravel paths led you to the canyons edge. No steel rails to keep you back from the edge. No, you could sit and dangle your feet over the canyon's edge if you had the nerve. And the scenery of the canyon was beyond words. I made sure to stay back a goodly distant, but Big Bird, and Ern ventured to the canyons edge in several places.

It was a GREAT DAY and we spent several hours there watching the walls of the canyon turn their many different colors as the sun's rays bounced off of them as it rose in the bright, blue, sky. No others where we were. No people, houses, cars. No, there wasn't even a breeze to disturb the silence. The only thing which could have improved this picture was if a Bald Eagle were to fly into it. On this day that wasn't to be.

"You gotta see this, Elmer," Ern's voice spoke into the silence. He walked beside me to a section where looking down into the canyon's depth you could see the Colorado River.

"Wow!" was all I could voice. From this distance, the river wasn't in color, instead it was a silver streak lining the canyon's floor, reflecting off it like a mirror.

Looking down into the canyon at the river, my thoughts went back to 1968 and our own River Journey and what we had spoken of about tubing the full length of the Mighty Mississippi River along with the Colorado River.

Although that never was to be, I have often sat and thought about it. What it would have been like to just let the Mississippi take you all the way to the Gulf, or letting the Colorado take you through the Grand Canyon. No thoughts given to the white water rapids.

Although hundreds of pictures were taken that day of our canyon visit, none would capture the picture I had in my head at that moment. Those thoughts I have had over the years were the same as I had today, only a memory of what could have been, but never was, nor could ever be.

The saying, *"All good things must come to an end,"* came about too soon for me that day. But, like the 60's! When they were over. They were over. It had been a great day but when it's over, it's over, and time to set Big Birds Tom, Tom on the Santa Monica Pier and journeys end.

CHAPTER 8

Driving from the canyon we made it back to Route 40, and to the last Casino where we would stay the night putting us within a four hour drive of the pier. I told Ern that we needed to be on the road early or we would never get into Santa Monica, so around 5:30 a loud knock on my door. It was Big Bird, and they were ready to hit the road.

"California," I heard Big Bird call out.

I sat up-right never realizing I had even fallen asleep, and saw the California State Line sign than just past it the sign for Needles, California, and then I found myself transported back in time to the back seat of an Eldorado Cadillac in the year 1968.

Needles, California that day was 114 degrees in the shade. One-hundred and fourteen degrees was etched into my mind so that fifty years later I can still recall it. A light bulb went off inside of my head with the thought of, why was the temperature so important for me to recall? For the temperature to be that high, it would have had to have been in late July or early August meaning we would have been on the road for at least four weeks.

This ride was only going to Barstow, but because we had helped with the driving, the driver was to take us to the oceans edge in Santa Monica. It was still early in the morning, and still dark out so I laid my head back down and let my thoughts take me wherever they wanted to.

As my eyes closed, I didn't know if I would reach the pier in an Eldorado with Dave in 1968, or with my two high school friends in 2018. As it turned out I arrived at the pier in 1968. The pier area, and the people there were different then I had seen pictures of, and read about, but it was now 1968 and what had become known as the Summer of Love, namely 1967 was over.

"Wake up, Elmer, we're here!" It was Big Bird who spoke and reached back and was shaking me awake.

Whatever I was dreaming was lost to being woken-up so suddenly.

Driving under an arched sign we were on the boardwalk headed to find a parking place. The pier was almost as windy as when we visited the Cadillac Ranch in Texas. It's hard to believe just how crowded it was here. The first thing on our agenda was to locate the sign marking the end of Route 66 which we did easily. There was a line of people waiting to have their picture taken under the famous sign. Waiting our turn gave me plenty of time to look around at the crowd on the boardwalk, of which many were of orient decent. I tried hard to visualize the scene here on our arrival in 1968 but drew a big blank. Maybe, I thought, before the day was over some memories might surface.

The Santa Monica Pier was everything we had read about it, and seen pictures/video's about, but with everything, nothing is as good as experiencing it firsthand. The pier was packed end to end with people young, and old, singles, and in groups. It was hot for being at the ocean with a constant breeze, or should I say wind blowing. No doubt, my hat would have been history if I'd worn it.

Ern, and Big Bird set out while I lingered behind. I have been here several times over the years since 1968, and it hadn't changed that much, sure they have made lots of physical changes but other than that it wasn't much different overall.

That is, unless you point out the people. Now! That's where the changes are.

Street Vendors or Pier Vendors were everywhere lining both sides of the pier with their carts, and tables. Everywhere there was a space it was taken-up with gift racks of some sort. Music was a constant as wanna-be-singers with guitars, keyboards lined up to be heard and to sell their CD's. I wondered if they had to pay an extra charge to be plugged into electricity. Being where this was my answer was, probably they had to.

As sated earlier, we waited to take our pictures with the End of the Trail sign, after which Ern, and Big Bird took off as planned. It didn't take too long to understand why Californian's preach tolerance, and expect everyone to do the same. Whatever pictures you have seen or that your mind can conjure up, well they were here. Men walking hand, in hand, women doing the same. Facial piercings, and tattoos. I lost count of the nose rings I saw that day. Mother's breast feeding their babies right out there in public on the pier. As if they were in the privacy of their liven rooms. Who would even want to do that?

And ladies! If you are going out in a wind storm wearing a short skirt or dress, please wear panties! That goes for all you grandmas, also! After seeing my 700 hundredth bare butt, my eyes hurt.

Food as well as the gifts were pricey. Of all the vendors on the pier I only saw two carts where there were brightly, colored, tye-dye tee shirts. Taking a bench where I could look out over the beach, I longed to have been able to descend the many stairs for a chance to walk in the sand, or as a well-known country singer puts it; "I've got my feet in the water, my butt in the sand." A group of young girls walking by on the pier wearing swimsuits made up of less material then that in my tee shirts pocket was getting whistles from some guys watching them pass. Looking out over the beach, I tried to visualize me being there back in 1968, but no memories surface.

No matter how hard I attempted to look into the past, it was for some reason shut out. There was a reason for this as I would learn later as we drove into the night, free from all of the days distractions. A pier vendor appeared in front of me with three gorgeous colored Cockatoos on his shoulders and head. For the price of ten dollars he would place one, of your choosing, on your arm, or shoulder for a picture. Believe it or not, within the matter of a few minutes there were about six people standing patiently waiting to get a picture.

It was easy to spot my two friends walking up from the beach, but I was the only one noticing them although they both stood out like the proverbial green-thumb. Once they arrived back up on the pier, it was, according to them both, *time to go.*

The original plans were to drive up either the Big Sur, or Route 5 to San Francisco, and cut across California on Route 80, but instead took Route 15 to Las Vegas, up to Salt Lake, and home on Route 80.

The vehicle was quiet on the drive out of California. I would later find out from both their take on what their experiences were on the pier in Santa Monica.

Driving through the night reminded me when as a child, mom and dad would tuck my sister, and I in the back seat of their car for the winter trip to Florida choosing to drive through the night when there was less traffic on the highway. We would winter in Florida where dad picked citrus, then summer in New Hampshire where he was a lumberjack.

I hadn't talked to my two friends what the urgency was to get out of California was which brought them to change driving plans, but later was told it was just the discuss with what they saw that day realizing how much different the California lifestyle was from theirs., and it was like they didn't want to be around it for fear some would rub off on them.

Somewhere in the middle of the night I was awaken by us stopping at a gas station. Hearing voices I got up, and had Big Bird open the back so I could get out.

I was going to go inside, but the place was closed although the gas pumps were on. It was freezing out, maybe forty degrees. By the time I relieved myself, I was shaking I was so cold. Big Bird got me a blanket, and I once again snuggled down to get some sleep. Where sleep evaded me, old memories didn't.

Lying in the dark all snuggled down, the first thing I heard was a voice calling out, California, just like I had heard in the wee hours of that very morning.

Next came the Needles sign. The difference now being, I was in the back seat of an Eldorado.

The next influx of information brought to light was I was in Barstow at an abandoned warehouse. This must be where we were delivering the piece of equipment to we had been hauling, except there was no equipment, instead, the U-Haul was packed with bricks of Marijuana. What I had always remembered, was just un-hooking the U-Haul inside the warehouse, and driving out. This was a completely different picture. The U-Haul hadn't been dropped off as I thought I had remembered, but offloaded. Out of nowhere several youngsters appeared and started pulling the bricks from the trailer emptying it in the matter of minutes. The back door to the Caddy opened and my friend stuck his head in, and tossed me a very large baggie of pot.

Seeing his smiling face put me at ease some. I had come to trust Dave's judgement although we hadn't known each other all that long. Up till this point I'd never been in trouble, and these thoughts entered my mind at this time.

If we would have been caught there surely would have been jail time. And what about while we were driving? What if we had been stopped by the Highway Patrol? Did he have weapons? Would he have pulled them out, and gotten into a gun fight?

I shuttered laying there in the darkness of Ern's vehicle with these thoughts. I was back to the present day.

"But we had gone undetected," I whispered low enough so I wasn't heard.

I thought for a moment how different my life could have turned out if that picture was painted differently. Why was I shown this at this time in my life? There is nothing I can change in it. I can't paint it over. Why hadn't I been shown this canvas before? Questions, questions?

I didn't have time to give this picture any more thoughts as others were being turned over. The picture my eyes were drawn to was the Santa Monica Pier.

As one would guess, it was lined with people, but they were different. The year was 1968, and wow, what a different a year had made. It seemed that the movement known as *The Summer of Love*, having started in 1967, and is what drew me and Dave to venture out to California in the first place had ended.

Very few in the crowd wore the hippie cloths I had come to love. Walking about the pier I picked up some of the talk of this new era although it was still the 60's. Gone was the peace signs. Instead a sign baring a raised close fist re-placed it. I saw the flag set on fire right there on the pier, action edged on by the hoots, and shouting's of the crowd which had formed a circle around the spectacle.

The music which had defined the 60's was replaced by the Heavy Metal, Acid Rock sounds, as bands such as Cream, Steppenwolf, Jefferson Airplane, and the likes. It appeared the all-around feelings I had come to love, at least here on the pier had been re-placed by those phrased by Timothy Leary…TURN ON..TUNE IN DROP OUT. I noticed the faces. Most wore a blank stare. Once happy looking eyes now seemed almost lifeless.

I would come to know that lifeless stare as, one, by one of my friends would become hooked on the hard drug known as Heroin. Heroin played the biggest part in ending the hippie movement in California to start with, then on the east coast, and slowly making its way across the US. Classifying myself a hippie, I soon realized I had either join them, or get out of Dodge sort-of-speaking. I had a good thought why I was now being shown that side of my trip of 1968, and why I had blocked it out.

The next picture I was shown was of the beach. I smiled as my thoughts went back to that time. I was there sitting in a small group of hippies, and taking in the sun, high on some good weed that was passed around, but we were the out-cast.

North of us in Haight Ashbury, and Golden Gate Park, they had a funeral titled *Death of the Hippie* at the end of 1967.

Why hadn't I paid more attention to the news and TV before leaving? I might not have if I would have known what was being revealed to me now. I wondered why my traveling companion, Dave wasn't in this picture, then I remembered him telling me he had met some girl and would be back in a couple of days, and to just hang out and wait for his return.

I told him I would stay around there for four days then I was headed to Sausalito, and he had the address, and phone number there just in case we had gotten separated. Spending four days on the beach, and seeing the faces on those others gave me an answer to one of the questions I have had for fifty years.

Four days later, Dave re-appeared with a girl in tow. The first thing I noticed was the cloths they both wore. This was followed by the stare on both their faces. It was the same lifeless, hopeless stare I had seen on too many faces over those last four days, and I knew than the changes Heroin has from that first boot on your body.

Sure it might give you the feelings of being in utopia, but the part of Timothy Leary's phrase *DROP OUT* becomes the part of you that physically shows, and although my friend might have been able to function the look he had on his face told another story.

Greeting each other as brothers, introductions were made between us all after which, we made plans to get on a bus the next morning to San Francisco where my brother would meet us and bring us to his home in Sausalito. I don't recall the girl's name, so I'll refer to her as Dawn. We spent the night on the beach the three of us. I was anxious to hear all about his travels and where he had been the last four days, but he wasn't in any condition to carry on any conversation.

As much as I tried to get myself and Dave back together, it never happened.

He, and Dawn stayed to themselves, gone was his belly laugh I had come to know whenever he let loose.

Meeting my brother at the bus station was the happiest of times. I had always put him on a pedestal, where I had to always be looking up to see him. He was my hero, my champion. He lived in California, had the fast cars, and women.

Nice apartment, art, and a stereo system that could vibrate your very being. When he would come back to New Hampshire to visit, he threw money around to all the family. We spoke often about me coming out to California to live, and to work together, and now here I was.

Later, after I was married the first time, he would come home with some of the best pot and Cocaine of the day, and I would get friends over and we would party, and yes! I still wanted to be just like him.

When he would visit when I was younger, I'd pick up his mannerism, and even his speech to the degree, my mom would sometimes call me by his name.

Why was I remembering all this now? I had the feeling this other side of the story, was one I needed to know.

Meeting my brother at the bus station in San Francisco was probably the happiest both he, and I, have been. The hugs were bear-like, and tears flowed on both our faces that day, and if I'd known that would be the last time we would ever hug, I might not have let it end. The talks we had in the past about me coming out west to live was going to be short lived.

Let me start by saying, my brother was not happy after meeting Dave and Dawn. I could see it in his face although he knew about them being with me. After arriving at his place in Sausalito, and giving them a room to sleep in, we went outside for a walk. Here, my brother told me they weren't welcome in his home. They were users, and he wouldn't tolerate them. Although my brother was a dealer he told me he wasn't a PUSHER! This started for me to see my brother in a different light. How selfish he was with everything he had, why I couldn't even play his sound system. If I wanted something I had to buy it, and then he would complain it wasn't good for me. He had lived his life the exact way he had wanted to, there was no room for someone else even if it was something we both wanted.

Where Dave and Dawn went, I never knew, and even after Dave and I got back together, I never knew, but that June day I walked into Sausalito Park, and saw Dave there I knew it was time to leave California if he was ready also.

We greeted each other like old times, then sat about on the grass smoking a joint. Dave seemed his old self. I saw that spark once again in his eye, but he refused to talk about anything of where he had been. I hadn't realized how much time had passed.

I had taken to hitch hiking all around the west coast which had caused numerous fights between me and my brother, and had caused me to move out, and live with some *head jerks* I had meet down at the park. I seldom saw my brother during this time, and those times became fewer and fewer. And here it was June of 1969 a whole year had passed me by.

Anyways, Dave was excited about an upcoming festival he had been told about from friends back in New Hampshire, and was headed home in time to go, and since he was, he thought I might like to go also. He was planning on hitch hiking and thought it would be like *old times.* Thinking back on that day, I don't remember hesitating at all before saying let's go.

I packed up a few of my things, and left the rest, gave my brother a call and told him to me in the park downtown. There were no hugs or tears only a very angry and "If you leave now, I have no brother!"

I did leave that day, and sometimes when he came home we would see each other, later we wouldn't see each other at all, and when he married I wasn't even invited. I truly wouldn't get over how much this all affected me till my second marriage, and to a woman who brought truth, and honesty back into my life.

All this I remembered at this time, but more clarity then I remembered it from the past. Dave and I had plenty of time to hitch back to New Hampshire for it was only June and the festival wasn't till August. What transpired would be *good-times* followed by *bad times* as two friends tried to capture some of 1968 in the year 1969

CHAPTER 9

The canyons we passed through were majestic. Ern had turned on the dashboard camcorder, and looking at those videos now, I'm glad he did, but they will not do them justice.

Traveling as I did, I have been through these canyons many times, and have hundreds of photos of them in the noon day sun, early/late evening when they reflect all the bright red, yellows, oranges, and blues of the sky which blankest them. I have never driven through them in the rain or the dawn of day, but have seen photos on-line. Second best thing from being there. How can some *not believe* we have a Supreme Maker?

"Beautiful, ain't it?" I asked neither one, just making a statement. It's funny how I had mentioned recently in this story about talking religion, and politics. I realized I knew nothing about Ern's, and Big Birds beliefs.

I was going to ask now, but for some reason my lips were suddenly sealed shut, the one thing I have learned over the years, and sometimes with dire consequences because I pried them open, was this, "When your lips get sealed shut, you leave them sealed shut."

If another time presented itself then I would surely talk to them about this, if not, then so be it. For now, I let my eyes take in all the beauty surrounding us knowing I would never see them again, and how wonderful it was, and had been seeing them with these two high school friends, which truly made for a memorable one.

We stopped from time to time in the many look-out areas which had been constructed every few miles, so visitors could pull off the road, park, and leave their vehicles to explore the area and to take pictures. We proved no different than them.

At one of these turn-offs was a plaque with a boy's face on it with the date he was killed on this spot. There wasn't a reason so, I took a picture so I wouldn't forget his name to do a web search to see what had happened to him. Ern, Big Bird, and myself, said he was probably drunk or on drugs and was messing around and lost his balance and fell over the edge.

It was a possibility but far from the truth. I did do a web search once I got home. Seems, one Christmas Eve, he and his girlfriend were coming back from some function when he lost control of his car, and it nosed dove over the canyons edge. He was killed, but his girlfriend lived. They were in the front seat, side by side, yet she lived, he died.

Ern, and Big Bird were in constant drive mode. Seemed they both wanted to get back to a more familiar territory. I knew their feelings. I had been there fifty years ago. And was on the way back to New Hampshire after a year away.

Wow! I remembered that 1st night on the road. Even though my brother wasn't happy, he drove us to the eastern side of Sacramento so we had an easy onto Interstate 80. It was my plan to get home as quickly as we could, but when I would hear from a ride of some happening somewhere, well both Dave, and I were drawn to go there.

I had remembered these times as good times with Dave being his old normal self after a day or two, but one has to remember I hadn't seen Dave for quite some time, and he still wouldn't speak of the past. This was a happy time once again for me. Had things been different between my brother, and myself…well who knows.

All I knew was the here, and the now, and I was happy once again.

From those who gave us rides I learned quickly that 1968 had given in to 1969 and the changing attitudes that was expressed towards those who were still hippies. The anti-war movement was on full swing all across the country, and although the hippie generation were anti-war, we were considered not vocal enough, those who stayed on the side lines. Maybe this we owed to; Peace, Love, Sex, Rock-N Roll, nice pot, 'shrooms, and LSD. The youth and demonstrators of 1969 were fueled by; Violence, Hatred, Heroin, Amphetamines, Hard-Lined drugs, along with a heavy metal sound in the music.

When we got a ride it was now more by the later teen ages as to the hippie ones. The hard-lined drugs scarred me. Not only because I knew at any minute might my will power give in to them, but because of the law. We were hitch-hikers, and more subject to *Johnny-Law*, stopping, tearing apart our back packs, and carting us off to jail for practically no reason. God forbid if they were to find hard drugs.

Yes! For sure the times had changed, but I wouldn't, couldn't. I did change though. You see, the 70's were different than the 60's with its turbulent 1969, and as I sat back and observed what effect these hard-lined drugs was having on tomorrows youth, and on my friend, I stayed scarred.

Just as pot was easy to get, and most of the people we had met on our trip across The Mother Road, Route 66, in 1968, so were the hard drugs of 1969. More of our rides had the later, and soon Dave had those lifeless, hopeless eyes I had witnessed on the beach in Santa Monica.

For the first time I didn't want to be around Dave or any of the ones we were sitting with. I remembered pulling Dave away from the fire that night, and telling him this. I remembered the torn feelings I had in doing so. What I didn't recall was in the morning he was gone, and the remainder of my time hitch hiking would be by myself. I wondered why this was hidden from me until now.

All the places I visited was alone where I thought Dave was a part of those visits also. So why? Why had this very important fact been kept from me for fifty years, and why reveal it now when I am writing a book that family, and friends were going to read, and probably show some discuses towards me although I'm not that person today.

I feel over the years I have used my experiences to better myself, in which I have although it would take me sometime to leave the past behind in its entirety. Laying there listening to Big Bird snoring, this all came back to me. Vivid pictures invading my mind at light speed so to get them all in, and recorded so I might see them, and remember never to forget again. I still didn't know all the importance these realizations were going to have on me if any. After all, it was fifty years later, and wouldn't have any effect on my life today.

There isn't one thing, no, not one second we can change once time has passed. And now a different thought entered my head. If I could go back in different times in my life, would I take a different path knowing the outcome of doing so?

This is a heavy question, I told myself. Let me explain that statement. What starts the journey down a particular path? Is it when you get to it? Will that path be different depending on what side of the bed you got up on that morning? Having a cup of coffee or not having a cup of coffee? Speeding to work or driving slow? Running the stop sign or stopping? Does the simplest of decisions effect our lives if we make the wrong one, and where does that action start? We all have said, *what if*.

What if we had only been two seconds later? What if we hadn't tossed that beer bottle out the window before looking in the rear view mirror? This could go on, and on. I will take it for granted you get my drift here about this subject.

A gas stop interrupted my thoughts, and I was glad it did. Believe it or not, this gas station was right out of the 60's. This was Route 80, and built much later.

Route 80 closely followed the Lincoln Highway, and when completed in 1986 it became the first highway across the US.

Although the station resembled one of the 60's it was a lot newer, so thoughts of pumping gas, or washing windows there vanished. Gas pumped, potty break taken care of, then back on the highway. I wanted to talk, but Big Bird had his eyes closed already knowing he would soon have to be behind the wheel.

For me, I don't even remember closing my eyes.

I didn't drive at night when I was working for that reason. I can fall asleep while driving if it's dark out. The thoughts, and dreams I was having before we stopped returned, but took on a different snap-shot entirely. I had always believed these hiking days were with Dave and me, I would learn this was not the true fact at all.

When I had awakened the first morning Dave was gone, in his place was a young girl I'll refer to as Donna. Donna told me she was eighteen, but I would question that today, and thank God we were never put in a situation where she had to prove it. Donna was what you would label a free spirit. All she wanted to do was have physical contact of some sort of another, and believe me, to her it didn't matter what. If we were with other people she made herself available to all. I don't think there is an overpass on Route 80 her and I didn't grace with our presence.

And me! Well! I thought I had passed on from this life and into another.

Be it guys or gals she had no preference.

"WOW!" I bolted upright in the back of Ern's vehicle. Hitting my head on the roof. My vocal, and the loud thump my head made hitting the roof, startled Ern who almost drove the vehicle off the road, to waking up the snoring Big Bird. All of this laid out in front of me. Complete contrast to what I had believed to be, and what I had always told it to be in my stories of the 60's.

"What the heck is going on there, Elmer?" Ern, and Big Bird questioned.

I was rubbing my head, and shaken at the same time. There was no way I was gonna talk about this, and here I am writing about it instead. Donna sealed my desires, and believe me, I didn't mind, that was until I met a girl who truly loved me unconditionally, and was willing to stand beside me through whatever it would take for me to get myself right, but when I ended up cheating on her I just couldn't tell her, so I walked away from her instead.

Here, what I had been thinking, dreaming about, and questioning, entered the picture. Here in black, and white was one of those paths that I could have taken which would have had a major impact on my life as well as another's.

I know now you don't bring someone right to the point of asking the question "will you marry me" then suddenly walk away without any reasons why without it having drastic effects on that person's life, and others around. Her family, my family, close friends.

Is this one of the reasons I have had this eye opening experience, at this time, was all about? I lay there and asked myself. *And if so. WHY? I can't change anything about that now?*

And writing about this now for all to read, and know about me. WHY?

The answer came to me over my next thoughts. There's someone who will read this that needs to hear it.

Or has he/she already?

Was remembering these instances from my past giving me some kind of advanced warning?

Being stricken with the many health problems I have been, and unable to drive, wanting to be able to travel but unable to, being offered addicting drugs of the day to help control pain was I being given some sort of advanced warning sign?

I didn't sleep a very peaceful sleep for the remainder of the trip home.

My wife just stuck her head in my door, and asked if I was still writing. I told her yes. My story had just taken an unsuspecting turn. If only she knew what sort of turn that was. I won't tell her though. She, just like you readers will have to read about it here on these pages.

As my eyes closed again I wondered what the end journey of this trip would reveal to me, and not only about the present, but my more recent Journey Back to the 60's.

CHAPTER 10

As I wrote down Chapter 10 a book title just came to me and one that reflects the writings on these pages. Right now I'm leaning to *BETTER LEFT A MEMORY*…It will have to be something a lot better that jumps out at me but this I'm pretty sure will be it.

What I had always remembered for the most part concerning the 60's and my involvement in it has been up till now shown to me as being something quite different than what my memories had lead me to believe. With truths being brought out into the open, not only for me but for readers, I was afraid to close my eyes again.

This newest picture acknowledged to me was a hard one to swallow. By including it here in black and white, it was for anyone to read, family, friends.

I became like those movie stars you have read about in the rag mags with all their dirty laundry hung out for everyone to see. I almost chose not to write this book once I saw the turn it was taken, but as I wrote previously, I feel there is someone besides myself who needs to hear this story.

I did finally fall back to sleep, but not before promising the guys I'd tell them what had brought on my out-cry. Although Dave had now been replaced by Donna, instances I had remembered back in 1968, and now 1969, were pretty much what I had remembered them to be.

Even as I write this, I really wonder what those truths really are. The things I have always thought them to be, or these new pictures I have been shown from that same time frame. And again. WHY NOW?

The next gas stop, I got out and took the front seat. It felt good sitting up instead of laying down, and my butt hurt from the makeshift bed. It was still night out so there wasn't anything to see, just some conversation with my friend.

Ern once again told me some facts about his life, offering up nothing that wasn't asked. I told him about my wife Marion and our family. My career choices, and the likes. It was just like old times talking to my friend even though not much was said. Just for the fact I was there in the front seat with a friend of over 50 years, for we had been friends in Jr. High also.

Big Bird woke up, and for what little he said, joined in the conversation. I knew for a short time, he had lived in Sausalito with my brother. I had never heard the whole story why he had left. I knew Big Bird had been married, and divorced, lived in Montana for a spell, operated heavy equipment, and had gone to Iraq with a job he had here in the states.

Both Ern, and I had been married before also. This was our second marriages, and both had already lasted longer than our first ones had. Although Ern was fairly new at marriage, he had been with his wife for a long time. Ern had followed a career path which he retired from. I had retired from the hot-water industry after a twenty-five year career spanning four states, and building four manufacturing facilities. A second career in the Spray-Foam Insulation Business and one spanning almost fourteen years ending with health issues would no longer allow my driving.

Small talk went on into the night between us. We talked families, Disney World, the need to get the family pool open. As we talked, I was hit by the realization there really wasn't much changed between us after so many years.

Jobs, and families had pulled us away from our home state, but that old saying popped into my head; *You can take the boy out of the state, but you can't take the state out of the boy.* Wherever we live, be it Indiana or Tennessee, we will always be New Hampshire-ites first.

Small talk was soon done. It still amazes me that someone who hasn't seen or spent time together for fifty years didn't have much to talk about, then we are guys after all, not a bunch of chatty women. Not talking, my eyes soon closed, and sleep, and dreams returned.

It was dusk. I wasn't exactly sure where we were. I say we because Donna was still with me. The only thing I remember was just finishing counting the 400 rail cars on a distant train. Turning to Donna I suggested heading for the overpass and hankering down for the night when a car pulled over with screeching brakes, and the back door came flying open. Once the dust had cleared, there stood my friend, Dave, outside the opened door. Having come to the conclusion of probably never seeing Dave again this was an utter shock to me. How much more intense was this trip of 2018 down memory lane going to get.

The past exposed to me so far was an eye opening one, and one I hadn't put all the pieces together yet. I see parts that I understand, and parts I don't understand, and now to have Dave re-enter the picture!

I wish there was someone who I could share all this with who might be able to give me some insight on it all, but I have no one, so I guess I'll continue to look at the pictures as they are shown to me with hopes of them all falling into place, so I can understand them, or at least partly so.

Right now the picture was of Donna, me, and Dave together once again along with the old couple whose car we got into. Their names were Harold and Toni. Funny, in my original book I couldn't remember their names, now they were as clear as if meeting for the first time, they ran a half-way home for run-away girls, and Dave had been staying with them as a handy man.

The front door opened, and Toni got out. Harold got out and threw our belongings in the trunk. Donna was already in the backseat. Dave climbed in and closed the door, which left Toni standing there waving me in.

Sitting between Harold, and Toni was a bit tight, but we made do. It wasn't more than ten minutes before moans could be heard coming from the back seat, and I knew what they were from. Donna was taking care of a constant itch. I don't remember that picture now with feeling of jealousy. No. For Toni had stuck a joint between my lips and lit it up, and at the same time ran a hand down…

Outside of being a half-way home for runaway girls, it could have mirrored a free loving hippie commune for which there were no rules, sort of a no hold back rule. If you could think it, you could do it here.

WOW! My brain shouted out from the front seat being woken up from what I was being shown in a dream concerning my trip of 1969 as I made my way home to catch the Woodstock Rock Festival, and re-meeting up with Dave.

It became difficult now for me to know when I was awake or asleep, in a real situation or an un-real one. What I had written about in the book, *Between the White Line and the Fence Post* was different than what I was being shown on this trip but this version of that long ago trip would surely shed light on the person I found myself to be once I returned home.

This painted picture would explain why I never could have one steady girlfriend, or for that matter, keep a marriage together, and it wouldn't be till I came face to face with my past would that ever change. If this was a

Porn Book I could fill up the pages with some pretty hot stuff, but it's not, so you just use your imaginations.

So! My brain once again cried out getting my attention. My eyes were open, and I was in the front seat of Ern's vehicle. It was still night time and the dashboard lights sat an eerie glow over its two front seat passengers. I turned my head towards the door so that Ern wouldn't catch a reflection of the dash lights off the tears that ran down my cheeks.

I had never understood, until now, why I couldn't keep that one girlfriend, or that marriage together, but now there it was all laid out for me to see. Now all that was needed was an answer to my question, "Why now?" The answer to my question either had been answered, but I overlooked the answer, or hadn't been answered yet.

My eyes were wide open now, but couldn't see the answer, instead they saw the dashboards lights reflected off of the closed side-door window. I turned to look at my friend, and realized how blessed I've been with two buddies of over fifty years to include me on this trip. I silently prayed they both got out of it whatever they desired.

In emails and Face Book chat with Big Bird, his answer to wanting to take this trip at this time in his life was a simple, and a straight forward one.

"Well, Elmer," he wrote. "This will be the last trip I will ever take here on this earth, in whatever lifetime I've got left." Simple answer.

Outside of wanting to re-visit Tombstone, and my beloved southwest, my answer would have been the same. I had a job that to me wasn't a job at all. Sure I worked for someone and collected a pay check, but also I got to travel this country. Planning my trips, as much as the actual dealer visit, but also around historical places in the area. I got to visit all those old western towns I write about in the many western books I have published. Walking their streets where famous gunfighters, and lawman alike walked. Standing face to face, eyes focused, gun-hand at the ready. Walked the streets which once knew the hooves of the cattle being driven through them. Streets alive with stomping boots, shouts, and hollers after the cowboy collected his salary and went looking for a game of cards, a drink, or to kick up a storm with a prostitute.

I have walked their streets. Drank their Sarsaparillas. I know I will never make a trip like this again, or even want to. I do have a trip in store back to New Hampshire to take part in my 50th class re-union this year.

I have contacted nieces & nephews I have lost contact with over the years, and all are excited to get together. One of those nephews, Steve, has volunteered to drive out to Indiana to pick me up, be my wheels when in New

Hampshire, and return me back home after the weeks end.

One thing for sure. Whole bellied deep-fried clams will be on the lunch menu.

High School friends will also be visited. I have a special luncheon sat with four dear lady friends whose names adorn one of my novels. Also while home I want to go visit my mom & dad. Something I didn't do enough of while living in New Hampshire. I know they will be looking down on me.

These were my thoughts now. These thoughts of returning home were a welcome breath-of-fresh-air sorta speaking. I would also see Ern again as he will be attending reunion. He had made the offer to pick me up if I needed a ride, but my nephew will pick me up, and be my wheels while in New Hampshire.

Here again, old thoughts re-entered my mind as I made contact with family, and friends I haven't seen in a very long time. I will visit with nieces, and nephews from my dad's side of the family as he was married before marring my mom. It has probably been sixty odd years since seeing some of them. After dad passed we quiet visiting that side of the family, so we lost contact until Face Book came along.

Now we are in contact and one nephew has even visited me here in Indiana. I'll see him again when home.

Sadly, his wife passed this year. I was blessed to have met her when he came out to visit this past year.

Why had these memories crept into my brain now for? I was still on our boy's trip down memory lane jogging between 1968, the 70's, and the present.

So. Was that the answer? Was the answer that simple? There could be no present without the happenings of the 70s, and no 70's without 1968.

"Can you imagine, Elmer? It's been fifty years," out of nowhere it was Erns voice.

"Yes, I can." I answered.

That's all that was needed saying. No further in-depth answer needed. *But was there?* This question was asked from deep within my brain, and as vocal as if it came from Ern.

Lightning bolts flashed inside my head as pictures from the past appeared and were flipped over before my eyes. So far the pictures were out of focus as they were turned over, but becoming clearer, and then the last picture landed on the pile. A picture so clear it was almost in real life instead of a photo. My Dad.

Immediately I knew where this was going so I closed my eyes, and took a deep breath and whispered softly, "Let's go."

CHAPTER 11

One might ask, where does my father fall into this story and my journey of 1968? Let me see if I can put it all together.

An argument I had with my dad in 1966 lead to me telling him I hated him, and I refused to speak another word to him even though we lived in the same house, so when I turned eighteen, and the day after my High School Graduation, me and Dave left New Hampshire for the west coast. Goodbyes were said between my mom and I, but not my dad, and even after I returned we didn't speak.

I had always said I was nothing like my dad, but right here, right now, I was being shown something entirely different. The reality of it was, I'm just like my father! This came as a shock to me.

Looking back on him sitting in his living room chair, I can even remember his right hand having a tremor to it, as he sat there drumming the arm rest. A spitting image to me sitting in my living room chair with trembling hand drumming the arm rest, crossed my mind. Early memories of always being wherever he was. Picture a puppy dog always under your feet. Well, that was me.

If he was in the garage building something, well there I was watching him, then later taking his instructions as he showed me the proper way to hammer a nail, or screw a screw, and to read a tape measure.

When I was young, we used to move to Florida in the winter months to get away from the cold winters in New England. As a matter-of-fact I was born in Florida. Dad would pick citrus, and there, right along beside him would be me under foot. My mom would tell me stories from those days, which always made me smile, and show me pictures she would take when she had the money to buy film. A cherished photo from those days, and one being shown to me now, was of a little boy standing in the open flap to a very large tent. I was later told it was an army mess tent. Also in the photo was about twenty black people, and some youngsters I used to play with.

You see, we were the only white people in the photo, and these folks lived with us in that tent. I played with blacks, ate with them, bathed together, and slept together. They were called *COLORED* throughout the country in the 50's. You have all seen the signs, NO COLOREDS ALLOWED.WHITES ONLY.etc, etc, etc. I grew up being non-prejudice in a prejudice country thanks to my father.

Although young, my memories have somethings they recall, like after a day of crop picking my dad would grab a 22 rifle and go shoot three or four squirrels which he would bring back to the tent where one of the women would clean them and throw into a large pot on the stove filled with boiling water. The stove could be moved either to be inside the tent, or outside depending on the weather.

The best tasting stews were cooked there by those colored women. The field's owner would often drive up and leave off a box with food in it. Some canned items along with fresh vegetables. And homemade bread, and usually a jar of honey which was a treat to dip little pieces of that homemade bread in.

I wondered now, if it wasn't for use white folk, if the field's owner would have still dropped off that food. Knowing what I do now, I would have to venture an answer of no.

A picture of me buying a burger and fries for the homeless person on the corner came into view. My desire to do so? Not really, but a learned behavior taught to me by my dad. My dad led by example. He didn't tell you what to do. He showed you what to do.

My success in manufacturing I owe a lot to rolling up my sleeves and showing an employee how to do the task at hand, not tell him how to do it. I have found there is a certain amount of respect you earn by doing so. Not wanting to be like my dad! Another instance where I was just like him.

Sitting there in the dark, with my head lowered, I felt a tear run down my cheek. At the same time, I whispered a silent, *thank you Dad.* I was showed many snap-shots there in the dark, some in black-and-white, others in vivid color. Here I saw a picture of my mom sitting at a table. Before her was a black-and-white photo. In front of her was a shoebox from which she removed a small tube. Squeezing out a small drop of its content, I watched her apply some to the photo, then carefully spread it around. Finally, she was satisfied with the results.

I watched her pick up the photo, and a smile came over her face. The same smile her face would get whenever she looked at my dad. Seeing me there, mom turned the photo, so I could see it. There looking at me was her wedding picture.

I still have that picture. It's in a stand-up frame on my book case. The only picture I have of my mom and dad. I've always wondered where the smile my face would get on it whenever my wife walked into the room came from. Now I knew, but it was from my mom, not my dad?

I'd never witnessed so much as an argument between them. Was it because whenever my dad looked at my mom, and wanted to say some harsh words to her, her smile overshadowed whatever he wanted to say?

Mom outlived dad by many years, and when I would visit her in the nursing home, and she spoke of joining him soon, that same smile would come over her face.

Why this picture? It was of my mom! Then it came to me as black-and-white as one of the photos I'd been shown. Without my dad, the smile on mom's face wouldn't be there.

A beam of light penetrated my closed eyelids, and I felt its warmth. A new day was happening right before my very eyes. Sitting there with the morning sun given me its warmth, pictures from the night wouldn't leave. There was dad giving me my first puppy. Another was dad's smiling face as he wheeled out a new bike I'd asked Santa for. There were many more. One with a go-cart. Another of me sitting in his lap. Little hands gripping the steering wheel as he let me think I was driving his car. In all these photos he wore a big smile. I wonder now, was it because of me, or was it because of the smiling face of the picture taker?

Dad loved this country and fought in both WW1, and WW2. He lied about his age when he enlisted for the first war. He was right at the age limit for the second where he was a Field Medic.

Dad's son, Bernard, from his first marriage, was in the Marines, and fought on Iowa Jima where he was wounded, and later awarded the Purple Heart. I have his Honorable Discharge paper someplace. I now have the need to dig it out, frame it, and hang it on my office wall.

I was shown a picture of me in my year book. There in black-and-white under future plans was a single word, ARMY. I never did go into the military, instead, armed with a 4-A Deferment headed for the west coast. You might ask yourself, 4-A? That's a sole surviving son deferment, and dad had another son, Bernard.

Bernard, after having a daughter was unable to have any more children which left me to carry on the family name which I've done. I have three sons, and a grandson, plus a granddaughter, so I'm covered…LOL.

So? I questioned again? And the answer came back loud and clear now. *As much as I said I would never be like him, I was just like him. I was truly my father's son.*

Mom and dad were only married for twenty-four years before he passed, and as I mentioned, I had never heard them argue. My sister told me one day after dad's passing, he was divorced from his first wife for Domestic Violence, so I guess he learned something if what she told me was true.

To be truthful here, I was shown a pile of photos in relation to my own life.

Photos that turned my stomach, and had me throw-up a little in my mouth.

I snapped my eyes open, so I didn't have to look at anymore photos, and was happy to find out I was still in the front seat of Ern's vehicle, and not in those photos any longer. A large Billboard got my attention, it was for the Bonneville Salt Flats.

"Hey, Ern, remember when we had talked about bring our cars out here, and we even thought about building a land speed special?" I questioned. "Whatever happened to that idea?"

"The Vietnam War, and life in general,"

The Vietnam War. As stated in my yearbook, I wanted a military career but because of my classification, that wasn't to be, which was probably a good thing as I would have been a war hero. As with most war hero's, they don't return alive.

I wanted to ask my friend about the war now. We had never sat around the table, or campfire, and talked about it. At least, with Ern I hadn't.

Here were some rare times I would go visit his mom, and dad, and while Chief was in the barn, Wally, and I would have some conversation concerning it and her fear for her sons. I wish there were more photos from those times, but I was shown none. The only snap-shot I have in my memory is her and I sitting around the table laughing profusely with tears running down our cheeks because of some story I had just told her about some strange date I had been on.

If Ern wouldn't have been my best friend, I might have asked his sister out, even though I'm pretty sure she would have laughed in my face, and that could have been a different path taken, a different set of photos to look at.

If Ern's sister ever reads this book, I know she will have a good laugh when she reads this, so will her husband as we were classmates, as well as friends.

I laughed inside at this vary thought, and at the same time wondered why I was shown this because here again, this path couldn't be gone back and walked upon in a different direction.

My mind searched for an answer to my question by turning over the many photos left to look at, and as the pictures on them were uncovered, and the pictures became focused, my eye saw there were many more questions in my searches that needed answers, or at least for right now they did.

Turning over a very large photo, I looked down on it, at first, with a questioning look on my face, and then with one of utter understanding. The photo was of me, looking up with a big smile on my face.

My answer was a simple one even when I was expecting a more in-depth one, it was simply to make me smile. I went back and looked for those photos I had turned over while searching out this answer. All the photos were of me wearing a big grin on my face, and they were all taken by my dad.

There was one of me holding up a brook trout on the end of my fishing line.

Me sitting on my mom's lap at the piano. Me holding up the keys to my first car.

Me with Patty going to a school prom. The pictures were fanned out there before me now, and too numerous to count or take in.

First smiles as I looked at the pictures, then sadness as I looked on them with the thoughts of not ever enjoying these things with any one of my boys. The enjoyment I missed out on of never being there to teach my sons to fish. Watching them in school plays. To sit in the stands and watch them run bases, catch a winning pass, or receive their diploma.

As I searched these photos, I asked to be shown why, after all, both sets of photos were in direct contrast to the others. Ones showing me and my dad doing all sorts of happy things together. The other ones showing me and my sons not doing any of those happy things together.

Why were one set of photos in black and white, while the others were in color? I stared out of the window at the passing scenery searching for the answers which I knew would come. Here the realization hit me that I did accomplish not being like my father, and nothing in the way I would have guessed.

CHAPTER 12

Driving through the day, stopping only for gas, and to use the restroom we made good time.

For any of you readers who have traveled through the mid-west you know there really isn't much to see unless you were into old west history which I was, but seeing we all wanted to get home we didn't make any unnecessary stops. In my work travel I've been to them all anyways.

It wasn't work travel, or present day travel I was recalling right now, but our travels of 1969 and our returning back east.

The photo was of a lone hitch hiker in the middle of nowhere, thumbing by himself. Wet, and hungry as it had been raining and being caught in the open. A closer look at the picture revealed the loner out to be me. It was plain to see by the look on my face I was upset about something, and why was I alone? Where was Dave? Donna? Harold, and Toni? And the half-way house?

The photos started to become clearer as the minutes passed by. Dave had left Donna, and me at the half-way house saying he would return in a day or two. While he was away, Harold, and Toni drilled me as to where he had gone. It was plain to see they were not happy with his being gone for some reason. When Dave returned, I saw once again the lifeless, hopeless look in his eyes.

The eyes of the Heroin user. Without any fanfare, he took Donna, and they disappeared into the bathroom where they emerged several minutes later with Donna taking on the same look as Dave had.

All at once I remembered the bedroom door opening up, and Harold, and Toni entered. Harold had a pistol in his hand. Pointing it at the three of us, he demanded we sit on the bed where he questioned us as to the where bouts of the money. It seemed Dave had taken a goodly amount of money he had found while looking through Toni's dresser. Retrieving some of the money, and flushing what was left of the Heroin, we were told to get out. Leave our stuff, and to get out.

I was upset with them both, and told Dave I wouldn't be continuing on with them. There wasn't a clear photo as to our going our separate ways, but it was obvious we had. I recall meeting back up with Dave in New Hampshire to hitch to Woodstock, but even now that picture could change. I guess I would have to wait and see.

It wouldn't be until later on that night when these memories returned, and I was shown another path in the road which could have had drastic results, not only on my life, but on Dave's. Dave and I hooked back up when I returned to New Hampshire. I found him at my house where he had been staying upon his return which was only a couple of days before I did. I wasn't at all thrilled to see him there, but at least he wasn't with Donna.

Here is where I could have taken a different path, but I didn't. Woodstock Festival was calling. I told Dave that after Woodstock he was no longer welcome in my house, and would have to live someplace else. We never did make it back to my place. You see, about halfway there, it started raining out, so I turned around leaving Dave to continue by himself. That was the last I ever saw of Dave, or at least the Dave I remembered.

By turning around that day I missed the greatest, most single happening, which defined the 60's, and the Hippie Generation. WOODSTOCK! Sure! The 60's had other defining moments. The assassinations of President Kennedy, Robert Kennedy, Dr. Martin Luther King Jr., and several others. The 60's had a man landing on the moon, artificial turf along with artificial hearts. All of these defining moments in themselves, but it was the music that has always set decades apart from each other.

I didn't understand hard drugs. All I knew about them was the effect they had on the human body, soul, and mind. How, by their use, you could have a happy-go-lucky teen one minute, than an empty, lifeless, teen the next. Not only that, but the death it brought with it. I turned my back, and my friendship on several friends back then who are no longer with us because of drug overdose. Could my friendship at this time in their lives had made a difference? I don't know, is that a reason I was being shown that here?

What would my life had turned out being if not for meeting a girl by the name of MJ who took me under her wing, loved me, and sat my feet walking down a different path? Would the path I had been on have led to hard core drugs, and death? Might have. I was surely headed in that direction.

Just like MJ could have chosen a different path, and by doing so, it would have had a profound effect on my life, so could I have chosen a different path and had a profound effect on another's life.

I have never been shown these photos in such clarity until now, and it saddened me that I didn't have the same foresight for my friends as MJ had for me.

Would there have been a different outcome??? Who knows??? But why show me this now? It will not change anything. *It's just to show you what taking a different path could have had on your life, and others. Not just your path, but the path someone else took for you.* Came the answer loud, and clear.

I hope Dave made it to Woodstock, and got everything out of it that the media broadcasted it to be. I didn't. When I got home, I found a couple of small painting jobs to earn enough money to return to the road for another year, but it wasn't the same. I had always believed that my hitch hiking days were spent with Dave as my companion, but obviously that wasn't true. Did I imagine I hitched with someone who wasn't there? Had age, and lack of memory scrambled up my time frame?

For the time being I'm really not sure. Oh! I thought I was! Now, not so sure.

I guess I'll have to wait and see if clearer photos are showed to me, after all, this front part of this trip has been an eye opener, I don't see where the back half will be any different. I wish we would have had more time on the return trip.

Being a western writer there are places I would have liked to have brought my two friends to. To me, the old west is an ongoing way of life. In just about any place you visit there is history exposed to your eyes. Rather it be through recreated towns such as Tombstone, and Deadwood to name a couple, but also by how little some of the present towns have changed. Just their names paint a picture in your mind. Cheyenne, Tucson, Dodge City, Abilene, and on, and on. Horseback riders down Main Street. Cowboys sporting both hats, and boots. Horse, and cattle ranches.

A horse still has to be broken like they did it one-hundred and fifty years ago.

Today country music is just as much, if not more popular. New country artist are popping up every day, with their music spanning centuries not just decades. For all these reasons is why I have always told folks, I was born in the wrong state, and in the wrong century.

Although cowboying hasn't changed much except gunfights in the streets, and stage robberies. This is partly why I wanted to have Ern, and Big Bird experience Tombstone. I knew with them growing up during the years that I had, they had to have heard of Wyatt Earp, Doc Holiday and the Gunfight at the OK Corral.

Knowing Ern wanted to capture some of the 60's for its historical place in time, he would also get that same feeling by walking the streets of Tombstone, and I was correct. We had all enjoyed Tombstone, ending with the Gunfight at the OK Corral, and Ern having his picture taken with the actors. In the past whenever I could visit these western towns, and walk their streets, it was sorta like the same feelings I got whenever I would go back and visit my home state of New Hampshire, and the city of Laconia where I grew up. I know as much about the history of these western towns as I do my own, probably more so.

I wasn't shown any different photos at this time, so I guess my writing this was because it was part of this trip without any hidden meanings. Maybe it was for you the reader, after all, much of what I've posted on my Face Book site has drawn lots of comments from you all, notably if you have been to the same place the photo was taken from, such as Winslow, Arizona.

It amazed me how many of you readers have been there. As I mentioned, I'm a western author with several novels in print. My health forced an early retirement so, I started writing and haven't stopped. I feel it has helped me a lot in keeping my mind sharp doing research, and my fingers mobile by typing. It would have been great to have had time to visit with some of my fellow western writers, and cowboy friends I know through social media.

I bring this up because we just passed the Cheyenne exit, and Route 25 N to Wheatland, Wyoming where one of them lives. Doug is a cowboy rancher thru, and thru, and one of my early Face Book Friends. He has even come out to visit me in Indiana. My plans was to return that visit, but time, and the fact it was 3:00 am in the morning prohibited a visit at this time. I have an open invitation anytime, and so does he. This as an almost textbook friendship right out of the 60's. It doesn't matter how long we had known each other, but just the fact we do.

I have several western writing friends on Face Book, some well-known, and others like myself. Whenever we find ourselves on chat together, we chat, sometimes I get a random phone call from Doug just to say hello. Doug served our country during the Vietnam War, he was a Tunnel Rat. He chatted with me about that experience. On his ranch he collects and re-furbishes old wagons. I would have like for Ern and Big Bird to have met him. Maybe if there is a next time, it will come to be.

I personally think the three of us should take a yearly boys trip someplace, but maybe pick one area and spend our time exploring there instead of trying to take in so much with such little time, although there are some places along Route 66 I'd like to re-visit again.

One event I know Ern and Big Bird would love is the Hot Air Balloon Festival in Albuquerque, New Mexico. I had scheduled a work visit there one year to attend it. It is one crazy sight, as the sky is invaded by balloons of all shapes, and colors. Photos don't do this festival justice but go online and look at photos from past festivals. It is amazing. Some balloonist offer rides, but I didn't take one, and now I would providing both my friends would also, although I really, really, hate heights.

I would love to attend an NFR Rodeo. I'm pretty sure they have a big rodeo here in Indiana that I'm gonna look into this year. I don't recall ever attending a rodeo before, but would love to be in the crowd when they open the gate, and watch a bucking horse reach for the sky with rider on-board. Feel the vibration of its hooves hitting the hard dirt. See the smile on the riders face upon hearing the eight-second buzzer.

"Hey, Ern. Ever attend a rodeo?"

CHAPTER 13

I opened my eyes just as we were crossing back over the Mississippi River into Illinois. I was well familiar with this area of Illinois. Being the mid-west technical representative for two spray foam companies I had many dealers in this neck of the woods, but that wasn't what I was recalling at this time.

The photo's I was being shown was of an empty shell of a building. No doors or windows, and a dirt floor needing cementing over. There was another building there which had some workers in it, and they were having their lunch. This unfinished building was located in University Park, Illinois and would be my home for the next eight years. It was here a company named Benson Pump would build a Spa Manufacturing facility named Seven Sea's Spa Co. In the building where the workers were eating their lunch, was also all the equipment they had purchased from the closed down Continental Leisure Co. in Connecticut.

Continental was another unfinished building with no doors, windows, and a dirt floor when I started there. After its closing, and the equipment being sold off to Benson Pump, I took a job offer to set-up manufacturing with this company in Illinois. It was during this time I experienced my first heart attack. I would work in Illinois till I was offered another position with a different spa company located in Tennessee, which would eventually lead me to be in Indiana.

What was I being shown these photos now for, I questioned? After turning over many photos and seeing familiar faces in them, some taken in Illinois, and some in Indiana, I came to the conclusion it was to show me that my success was built on the combined talents of others.

Workers who I had hired, and trained in Illinois would later, after I tracked them down, re-locate and come to work for me in, Indiana, along with others who had been employed by a spa company in Indiana who now came to work for me also, all adding to my being able to concentrate on getting a building set up.

My wife, and both my step-children would eventually relocate to Indiana where I gave them both jobs. They both would meet their spouses there, and give us six grand-children. We have been blessed with them always living within a mile and a half of us. Kev, who is the International Sales Manager, travels the world. Karen, our daughter, retired this past year as Office Manager in charge of Dealer Accounts. The company has been blessed with having Michael Philip's as our Spokesperson, where a complete line of swim spa has been developed in his name.

As we crossed the Mississippi, the sun reflected its shimmering, silver rays off of it that pierced the eyes all the way to the back of the brain. No new memories or photos were showed to me. I just felt a sadness concerning my friend, Dave, and the plans we had talked about.

I would have loved to come back here to the Mississippi River, built another raft, and to lazily float on down the river all the way to the Gulf. I wonder how long it would have taken us. Would we have seen it through? Knowing the way we both were, I'd like to think we would have.

Now! The Colorado River would have been something else entirely. It's funny. How you don't think of something in fifty years than some long, lost, buried memory is awoken, and it was as clear as though it happened yesterday. The photo I was being shown was hazy, and blurry, but as my eyes focused in on it, it became clear. It was of another bridge by the Franklin High School, and it was a couple of years upon my return. There was a house down in a hollow next to that bridge where I was being taken to make an LSD purchase. You could have bowled me over with a marble upon seeing Dave on the other side of the opened door.

Until just this minute, I have had no recollection of seeing Dave once we separated for Woodstock. Maybe it was because I was staring into those lifeless eyes again, and turned my back on him once again. Although I could deal in LSD, Pot, Speed, and pills, I just couldn't deal being around the hard drug Heroin. I lost some friends to the needle, and wonder now, if I would have been more of a friend to them, and tried to help them as someone did me, would they be alive today? I don't know. I've not been shown that photo yet, and it's one I don't want to see. I hope I can just live with knowing what I do about Heroin Addiction now, although it probably wouldn't have made any difference.

These thoughts and photos I have been having and seeing were so long ago, most had been forgotten till now, when I was shown them.

But why now? This is the unanswered question I keep asking myself two months after getting back home from our 50 year, Route 66, Boys Trip. I have been out of the drug scene for longer than I can remember, but it was around 1972 when I thought I was finally out of that era in my life.

I had made plenty of money, was driving the car I wanted, and I was taking care of my mom as dad had passed in 1971. I should have been more careful. Having a brother come to visit who always brought with him the best pot, and lately Coke, the writing was on the wall as to how long my dry spell would last.

I thought about buying a house, getting married, and starting a family all of that was history. But I was horribly mistaken.

Just as an, *old boyfriend*, can come back into your life and threaten your future, so can old friends, a hemp plant, and a line of Coke. I was shown that even moving to another state, taking a really good job, and a chance to completely start over, that you! And only you have to want it, and faced with a marriage already in trouble, well, *I want it,* just wasn't there.

Seeing the glow the dashboard lights put on Ern's face, and hearing Big Bird snoring, soon had its effect on me, and once again felt my eye lids slowly descend till all was dark once again in my mind. If I get you a little confused with my nights, and days here, it is because we just drove except for fueling up, and maybe buying two eighteen hour old hot dogs off the hot plate in the convenient store or truck stop we fueled up at.

As much as I was hating to see our trip end, I was also thankful as I was pretty much in constant pain now. As my eyes closed another photo was turned over. I stared at it and thought what a strange photo. For a minute I remembered seeing many like it. Oh! The subject matter was different, but the over-all appearance of the photo the same.

I had seen lots of mom's photos where half was in color, and the other half, black & white. Here was the picture of a split in the path where you had to make a decision as to which way you wanted to go not knowing what you might encounter along the way. But this photo was different. One fork was black & white, where the other one was in color. Was this my mom speaking to me from the eternities?

Was she showing me what path to take based on her knowledge of the future?

And what about me? What life did I want to live?

If I read the photo correctly, by taking the path that was black & white would this indicate a life where everything sat out before me the answer would be in black & white, guaranteeing I wouldn't stubble and fall, or fail?

Where the colored path, although it was bright with color, there were also lots of shaded areas of gray, and even deeply colored ruts of black. As much as I wanted to choose the path where my life would be structured, and sure, I knew that came with a price. What fun would there be to life if you always knew the outcome of your choices in advance? Every time you jumped aboard that surf board you knew it was going to end with you catching the perfect wave, riding it onto the beach with the admiration from onlookers.

Wouldn't it be more fun to have jumped upon that surf board not knowing if the wave you catch was going to launch you into the air, dunk you under the water, and have you surfacing to the clapping, and shouting of onlookers?

My question here was, *at which fork in my life did this one photo represent?*

The answer was pretty much in black & white? This fork in the road simply represents all those times where you have to make a decision. It can be a simple decision or a major one. By being a fork, it makes us stop before continuing which forces us to look ahead with what we have been taught by our parents, teaches, and the Word of God.

I believe we are all born hard-wired with a moral compass which helps us make those decisions when called upon to do so. Rather or not we listen to the answer, and follow it, it's our decision to make, and our consequences to pay.

Believe me! Sooner or later there will be a price to pay, and what determines that price is anybody's guess.

Unlike the laws of the land which we are given in advance, so we know what the consequence is going to be if we make poor decisions, so are the laws we are given in the Good Book.

I'm sure there have been consequences I've paid without ever knowing what it was for. I tried really hard to clear my thoughts of everything except what I was being shown here. Gone from my mind was the sounds of the car's tires as they sung their song over the black-top. Gone, too, were the glowing lights from the dashboard, as well as the loud snoring sounds coming from Big Birds mouth. Once I did this, the photos took on a different image.

The path I had been following was shown to me as my walk through life, and believe it or not, had turned into

The Yellow Brick Road. What struck me the greatest was how many "Y's" it contained, and each "Y," or fork in the road, had one path in black & white, one in color, but they both joined back up with *The Yellow Brick Road* representing my walk through life. Just the volume of "Y's" were staggering that's when I saw clearly what some of them were.

Not all forks were major ones! But, ones that still required a decision, but not life changing ones. These "Y's" were just personal choice ones. Should I have bacon & eggs, or waffles for breakfast? Life changing? No. But still a decision to make. Some were eye openers, and ones we pay little mind to at the time such as, the difference thirty-seconds would make as you let that truck enter from the intersection that morning. Sure you got aggravated by the horn blowing behind you, but had you not stopped those few seconds, that car under the tractor-trailer truck you just passed might have been you.

I could feel my head wanting to explode. That explosion came in the loud snore from Big Bird which startled both me and Ern. I think I reached back and cuffed whatever part of his body I could reach.

All being awake, we pulled into a truck stop for fuel, restroom, and yes, the nine-hour old, two for $1.00 hot dogs, and to re-stock the cooler with Diet Pepsi and ice. I brought with me a DC to AC power converter, and wished I'd brought the coffee maker. Truck stop coffee is the worst coffee in the world unless it's made fresh. No nine-hour old hot dogs here, but two slices for $1.99 of ten-hour old pizza was on the menu.

CHAPTER 14

It was morning time now and we had just crossed into Indiana. It didn't seem possible that just eight days ago we were crossing out of Indiana. I learned that while in Michigan, Ern had ventured down here into Gary on several occasions.

"If only we would have known, Ern," I told him. Gary is only two and a half hours from Fort Wayne, and if you traveled there on Route 30 you passed within two miles of my house.

We three made small talk as we drove over familiar blacktop and spied places Ern and I recognized.

I recalled the story when I had to go to Fargo, North Dakota in the middle of the winter to do a spray-foam demo. I drove a Chevy Silverado Duelly, with a fully outfitted twenty-eight foot fifth-wheel spray trailer. When I hitched up my spray rig that morning it was almost blizzard weather conditions, but I didn't mind driving in any type of weather.

I've always been sorta of a fearless driver, I think that's one of the big reasons they chose me to head-up that new program. I've pulled that rig through forty-eight states at different times of the year, and was only involved in one slight accident being rear-ended in California at a stop sign, and stuck in the soft grass of a breakdown lane where I needed a wrecker to pull me free. I put 387,000 miles on that Silverado in six years. Until this trip I thought I had seen everything in this country I wanted to see of importance.

But like I said, I'd never been to Lincoln's Tomb, and the wild burro's in Oatman, Arizona, I had never seen before along with a few other historic sites which were listed in Ern's Route 66 travel guide.

Small talk out of the way, and Big Bird in the front, I once again closed my eyes. Different photos were flipped over before my minds eyes. Places were replaced with people, most were young, but I still recognized them from my youth. All photos I looked at were from my dad's first marriage.

When we were kids, and my dad was still alive, we would visit them almost every Sunday afternoon, and those visits stopped after he got hurt and could no longer drive or ride in an auto. My half-brother, and two half-sisters have passed, but through Face Book several nephews, and nieces have been located, and this September when I return to New Hampshire for my fiftieth class re-union, visits have been arranged.

One photo was taken last year when one of my nephews came out to visit with his wife. It had been many years since we had any contact, so this visit was a very special one. Shortly after they left my nephew's wife passed on. It was here that I noticed it. Although there were pictures of him and I, there were none of the three of us. For that matter I didn't even have a photo of the two of them.

How could this be, my mind questioned? *Now it's too late*. It answered.

Having been shown this, I made a mental note when I'm with my family, and friends in New Hampshire to take plenty of family pictures including those of their spouses. My wife and I were blessed in knowing her, and will get some photos of them both.

I want to get marriage photos of all my nieces, and nephews along with their families. Maybe I'll put together some coffee-table family photo albums when I return home, but then again they might not want to go back into the past. Maybe old haunting memories reside there they don't want to revisit.

I know this trip opened my eyes to some facts I had forgotten and buried long ago, hoping, I guess, never to remember them. And still I have the unanswered question as to why expose all this now when nothing newly learned will make one difference in my life now.

Is it because as I face the end of my own life I want to know everything about my past? I know for a fact, there are questions that only my mom, or dad could possibly answer, and their gone now. These questions will forever go un-answered, so why bring them up now? Even this question is one I have no answer for.

Maybe I will be with a family member who has some of the answers I seek. I know I will be paying close attention to our conversations, to see where they may lead.

If I haven't wanted to know all there was to know about my family when they were alive to give me the answers, why now when there is no one left alive who can?

A loud warning buzzer just went off somewhere in the depth of my mind, warning to be very careful what I might ask of others. I know, or should I say, I've always had a feeling there are some dark, unspoken words concerning my families past. *Do I really want to know what they are?* I guess I will just have to wait till the time comes, and pray for discernment before opening my mouth, something I haven't been real great about doing in the past.

Family members, and those who know me, know me as a straight shooter, and someone who will give you an honest answer no matter what. I feel if a person ask you a question they deserve an honest answer, and trust your friendship to give them just that.

For me anyways, there should be no gray areas where the truth is demanded, and for what I've been shown so far on this trip, I've given a lot of gray answers to my questions growing up, and even to what I had remembered from my first trip across Route 66 back in 1968.

Your mind is awesome, and through having many health issues I've learned just how awesome it is. Stroke patients, such as myself, who were paralyzed through therapy can train another part of their brain to take over the part that was effected, so they can regain movement, speech, and the like. Your brain can also shadow over and hide something that it feels is a threat to your existence, or would impair you in some way or another.

I'll give you a perfect example of this. For the longest time my sister always wanted to be a nurse DR. Not graduating high school, she studied day and night to get her GED, than studied some more to pass entry examines in to a good nursing school. I don't recall the whole jest of the story here, but she failed getting into the school because her eyesight was so bad.

This rejection, and a lifelong dream destroyed, she willed herself blind. She spent months in the Mass General Hospital while he doctors ran all sorts of test to determine why. It took a shrink to figure this out, and once she did was able to bring sight back my sister. Going blind was my sister's way of being able to live mentally stable with the rejection.

Were there memories so painful or destructive in my past my brain had hidden them so deep in hopes of not being found?

It was as though I had been shown some gray areas in my past, now I wanted to see those areas in living colors, and was searching out an avenue to do just that.

This thought would help explain why I have been having trouble putting the past in order or a correct time frame. My brain was coloring in with vivid colors all those gray areas, and giving me the honest answers, and details to occurrences, I, up till now, thought I knew.

As some photos were colored in, others would be exposed, and so on, and so on. Never overloading though. If my brain felt it was close to that happening, it would simply turn over a different photo for me to look at, and that photo didn't have to fall iconological order. This explains a lot why I might be remembering a certain instance, when something else I might see through the cars window conjures up some other memories.

Now I got a better understanding why when I saw a sign for Richardson, TX., my thoughts went to 315 Richardson Street, Sausalito, CA., because that's where I lived with my brother, and that would un-lock another wave of lost memories. Armed with this new bit of information, whenever a thought popped into my head, I just relaxed so it could mature, and expose some new information about the past.

It was as though at these times, my brain was forcing these memories to surface, so I would finally have to face them even though their truths couldn't change the course in my life, or the paths I chose to walk down, they needed to be exposed.

It would appear so much of my life had been lived on lies, even my beloved 60's along with my hitch hiking adventures. All the fond memories brought to surface had turned into something completely different than what I had stored, and re-told countless times.

Whammmmmmmmmoooo! An explosion of the brightest, white light went off inside my head sending lightning bolts to penetrate every corner of my brain. The suddenness of it would have dropped me face down to the ground if I'd been standing up. Even though knowing the truth now couldn't change anything, I needed to know the true facts surrounding my life.

What I hadn't been shown, was what my life would have been if I would have known the truth, and had dealt with it. Where I'd be if I'd taken a different fork in the road? Is this a picture that was trying to come out?

Realizing I had been shown lots of truths, but that was all I'd been shown. I hadn't been shown how my life might have been affected by my choosing to walk a different path. If I'd have taken a left fork instead of the right one.

My thoughts were blowing around inside my head at hurricane speed, so I needed to slow them down, and sort them all out. Another thought came into view here also. The thought was this: let's say, I took the path the day I was going to the Woodstock Music Festival that turned me around to go back home instead of going to the festival. If I'd have taken the other fork instead, would it have taken me to the festival, or would it have taken me back home also. This resulting in the same outcome. MISSED FESTIVAL.

You see both paths had the same outcome. *But, would the journey have been different?* Is that what I'm being shown here on this trip? Two different paths whose journeys were different, but shared the same outcome? Was it even possible to take two different journeys and have them lead to the same outcome?

The answer here was quiet clear. Of course it is, and I'm a walking, talking, living example to contest to that fact. My thoughts were stalled as the vehicle came to a stop.

We had entered Columbia City, and now only about twenty minutes from my home, and the end of an amazing journey. It had been an amazing journey. How many of you readers have had the opportunity to return to the same spots you had walked fifty years ago?

Every mile that we were able to travel on Route 66, I had traveled over the same blacktop fifty years ago. I might not be able to recall those exact miles, but non-the-less, I traveled over them.

The two different journeys I was shown had the same outcome. One of these journeys was real, the other wasn't. Although it was plain to see now that in life it is possible to take either the brightly colored path, or the black & white one, both can have the same end results.

In our walk through this world we face many of those forks. Many will be colored, and many will be black & white, and depending on which one we choose will determine how difficult the walk will be. Sometimes in my walk, when faced with that fork, I've been color-blind.

I'm a firm believer in destiny. I believe we are here for a planned and purposed walk through this life, and it's a walk that at times will be black & white, and at times colored. As we choose the path we fell is the right one for us we need to stop-before- go, and if given the time weigh the importance of what you want the outcome to be, and how difficult you want that journey to be. It is our human nature to want to take the black & white path, and to try to color it in as we see fit for us, this is when we get ourselves in a tight jam. We paint ourselves into a corner, sort-a-speaking, and don't know how to get out.

The black & white path will always show you what the consequences for your actions will be if you choose not to follow the path. If the speed limit is 55 miles per hour, and you choose to drive 80, you know, if caught, you will receive a speeding ticket, but you color that in by saying to yourself… *I won't get caught!*

And you might not get caught this time, which only fuels you to keep speeding until you get caught or have an accident. Believe me! That will happen in the end.

You must-not attempt to use color on that black & white path if that's the one you choose when faced with a fork in your life. You can only visualize the end of the path, and of course it's whatever you want it to be. What you can't visualize are all the turns, and bumps you have to take to get there. Some turns will put you into a ditch, some bumps will leave you bruised, and bloody. It's how you get out of the ditch, and how you bandage up those bloody bruises that determine the outcome.

I've learned to walk through life carrying two things…A, Triple-A-Card, and a box of band-aides. My Triple-A-Card has phone numbers of family, and friends, Pastor, Consolers, and others who I can count on to pull me out of the ditch. And the band-aides? Well, you just put them on yourself as you need them.

It would have been great to have had some time when I got home for the three of us to just sit outside, into the night, around the fire-pit, and just reminisced about our trip, but that was not to be. Maybe when we all get together in New Hampshire for our 50th class reunion we will have some time for that. This will give me some time to make heads-and-tails to what I had just experienced.

Another question I'm left to try to find an answer to is this. Which journey was the real one? Was it the one I've written about in; Between the White Line and the Fence Post, or the latest version of that trip?

In reality it really doesn't matter seeing it can't be changed in any form or matter, but knowing myself, this will bother me till I'm laid in the ground.

CHAPTER 15

The drive from Columbia City to my house was driven in silence. As Ern pulled into my driveway, turned the key off, and the engine was silenced, it truly marked the end to an incredible journey.

The three of us had just completed what many of you have probably dreamed about doing but never have, or for that matter, ever will. We might have missed some stops along the way, but non-the-less had just completed our MOTHER ROAD experience.

Until this trip, I never realized the impact the one of 1968 had, had on my life. Being home would give me the calmness and time to re-look at all those photos I'd been shown for the first time, and even some I'd seen before, but now colored in some.

On this trip there wasn't one mile of Route 66 I could say I remembered from fifty years ago other than the Twin Arrow Truck Stop, and probably that was because I have stopped there many times over the years. It would have been great to have remembered those different gas stations I'd pumped gas in. To have taken lots of pictures of the different places we had hitched to, especially our Mississippi River Raft Adventure.

I have only one picture of my friend Dave from back then, today along with all the pictures taken by Ern, and Big Bird I have over a thousand. The beauty of digital camera phones. I will put together a photo album for each of them to have a history to show friends or just to open from time to time and remember the day three friends of over fifty years sat out on an awesome adventure to reclaim some of the past.

I look at how our lives have changed over the past fifty years. How our bodies have aged, and can relate that to the Route 66 of fifty years ago to what it is today. We can return to familiar places from our youth, but when we do, we have to expect to find many changes there, and in some cases the things that were there no longer exist. Now gone just like we will be someday.

As the years have passed, so has Route 66. Each year it gets less and less.

There will always be those parts of Route 66 that will stay Historic thanks to a few who wants to keep the past alive. Sometimes I wonder if we try too hard to hold onto the past. We bury our dead in large, beautiful structures such as Lincoln's Tomb for all to visit, or Marilyn Monroe, James Dean, or Elvis Presley. It seems we can't let the past go completely. There is something that keeps our interest with being able to re-visit that which has died years ago.

I think those who have been able to face their own mortality are the ones who have themselves cremated, and their ashes thrown to the wind, their smiling faces remembered in a photograph, not a slab of granite sticking out of the ground.\

It is my opinion, and mine only, if a state chooses to de-commission a highway such as Route 66 then it should go in and tear down any structures that are reminders of it. I hope that never happens, but just saying.

It would have been sad not to have seen the Rainbow Curved Bridge, or the dilapidated truck stop at Twin Arrows, and the memories they conjured up.

We tend to want to remember, and hold onto those things, and times that we choose are important to us or ones that bring a smile to our faces whenever we recall them. All others become blackened shadows.

This was an awesome journey!! It appears I can't state that enough. I still have a boat-load of unanswered questions, but as time has passed they become less, and less important to get answers for. It makes no matter anyways.

You can't go back and change one thing! No. Not even one second…

The End

EPILOGUE

What a difference fifty years had made. Gone was ninety per-cent of the original roadway, bulldozed under, and newly paved over. Gas stations whose gas pumps with holding tanks full of gas to give more life to the autos who needed it.

Pulling into a gas station of today, I realized I would starve to death if having to rely on pumping gas today. Not only were the pumps all self-service with their credit-card canners, and user friendly pump handles, and the windshield washer buckets mounted on the island. So you could wash your own windshield, but you could go inside and purchase food, and drink.

Let's don't forget the electric box you can park next to, get out and pull a cord from your trunk, plug it in, scan your debit card, and wait for a half-hour, un-plug and continue on their journey. Yup! What a difference fifty years had made.

Only a handful of the old buildings exist today, kept alive by someone who refuses to let go of the past, and determined to educate you to it.

I had just completed the journey of a lifetime. You could say it was fifty years in the making. On this trip I was shown two sides of my life, now it was up to me to sort those sides out, and get their meanings as they relate to my walk today.

It has taken fifty years for me to get to this spot in my life, and who knows, I might never get the whole jest to this trip, and the many different pictures I was shown.

If you really want to know the truth! I don't know if I really want to.